QE2 Deck Plans.

Signal Deck, Sports Deck, Boat Deck
Upper Deck and Quarter Deck are not in scale.

Deck Signal

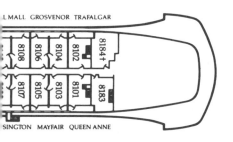

L MALL GROSVENOR TRAFALGAR

8108 8106 8104 8102 8184†

8107 8105 8103 8101 8183

SINGTON MAYFAIR QUEEN ANNE

Deck Sports

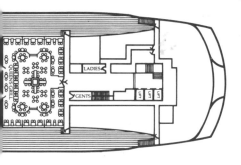

QUEENS GRILL

LADIES

GENTS

Boat Deck

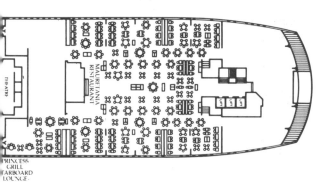

THEATRE

MAURETANIA RESTAURANT

PRINCESS GRILL STARBOARD LOUNGE

Upper Deck

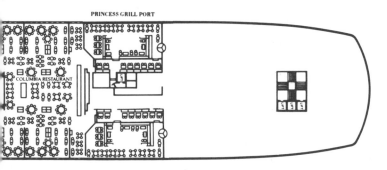

PRINCESS GRILL PORT

COLUMBIA RESTAURANT

Quarter Deck

(Continued on back)

QE2

CAPTAIN RONALD W. WARWICK

With a Foreword by H.R.H., the Prince Philip, Duke of Edinburgh

W. W. NORTON & COMPANY
NEW YORK • LONDON

To John & Helen
Bon Voyage on QM2
RWWarwick
Commodore ~ 14 Jan 05

The text of this book is composed in Cochin
with the display set in Kabel
Book design and composition by Guenet Abraham
Cover illustration © 1998 by Gerald Brimacombe

Library of Congress Cataloging-in-Publication Data
Warwick, Ronald W.
QE2 / Ronald W. Warwick ; with a foreword by H.R.H. the Prince Philip,
Duke of Edinburgh. — 3rd ed.
p.   cm.
Includes bibliographical references and index.
1. Queen Elizabeth 2 (Ship)   I. Title. II. Title: Queen Elizabeth the Second. III. Title: QE two.
VM 383.Q32 W38 1999
387.2'432 — dc21 98-46901

ISBN 0-393-04772-5
Printed in Hong Kong by South China Printing Co. (1988) Ltd.
W. W. Norton & Company, Inc., 500 Fifth Avenue, New York, N.Y. 10110
www.wwnorton.com

W. W. Norton & Company Ltd., 10 Coptic Street, London WC1A 1PU

2 3 4 5 6 7 8 9 0

CONTENTS

This book is dedicated to my father,

Captain W. E. Warwick, C.B.E., R.D., R.N.R.,

commodore of the Cunard Line and

first master of the *Queen Elizabeth 2*, and to

all those who have served aboard the liner.

There are those that go down to the sea in ships and make

their living on the oceans of the world.

These men see the works of the Lord and his

wonders in the deep.

PSALM 107

FOREWORD TO THE FIRST EDITION

The Cunard liner *Queen Elizabeth 2* was laid down just as the world entered a period of rapid technological development, and suffered some of the penalties of innovation. She was completed just as the era of the great North Atlantic passenger liners was coming to an end, beaten by the faster and cheaper liners of the air. Fortunately for her, she found a new career in cruising, although, at least in one respect, she followed the tradition of her predecessors by acting as a troopship. Among much other detailed information, this book describes her crucial part in the successful Falkland Islands campaign, which is likely to remain the most dramatic episode in an already very full career.

H.R.H., the Prince Philip, Duke of Edinburgh

When asked by Captain Warwick to write the foreword for this new edition of his remarkable book about the *Queen Elizabeth 2*, I jumped at the chance. Here was an opportunity for me to comment on an international icon, the most famous ship in the world, and on the man himself, an icon who loves her and knows her best. What an honor for me.

The world's vast oceans have fascinated me since boyhood, but my fascination has always been with the stately liners that ply the seas and the men and women who dedicate their lives to them.

I have indeed been a fortunate man. My professional career has allowed me to indulge my high interest in ships and shipping, and now my role as president and chief executive of Cunard Line Limited provides me with close and personal association with one of the oldest and most enduring symbols of British seamanship and the heritage and tradition of British excellence.

The Cunard name is known and honored throughout the world, and certainly Cunard's legendary *QE2*, as she is affectionately known, is one of the most enduring symbols of maritime greatness.

Captain Warwick's intimate history of this great vessel is alive with personal detail. As a master of the *QE2*, he knows every inch of every deck of his ship, as did his father, who, you will read in these pages, was the *QE2*'s first master.

His great love for the *QE2* shines through the pages of Captain Warwick's book, as does his admiration for staff and crew. A friendly and gregarious man, as well as a master mariner, Captain Warwick has hosted thousands upon thousands of *QE2* guests over his years in command.

Now the magnificent *QE2* has entered a new era in the long and honored history of Cunard. In May of last year (1998), Cunard came under the direction of America's Carnival Corporation, which acquired a controlling interest. Carnival's family of cruise lines is generally regarded as the most successful in the world. At that time, the venerable Cunard Line was merged with the certainly much younger but renowned Seabourn Cruise Line. The result was the formation of a new and vibrant company — Cunard Line Limited. And so a new chapter in the life of the *QE2* had begun. All of us who love her will realize that there are times when some change is necessary to maintain important continuity. The new Cunard Line Limited provides change while at the same time assuring this important historical continuity.

We are all happy that the *QE2* lives on and will continue to delight her shipboard guests.

Captain Warwick has done all of us a great service in telling her story.

Larry Pimentel
President and CEO
Cunard Line Limited

ACKNOWLEDGMENTS

I extend my appreciation to Robin Ebers, Eric Flounders, James Mairs, Gerald Brimacombe, Michael Gallagher, Nigel Long, Mike Moon, Simon Ranger, Kevin Boag, and Captain Robin Woodall for their advice and assistance.

I am also grateful to the members of the ship's company of the *Queen Elizabeth 2* who made important contributions.

A very special thanks is due to my wife, Kim, for her never-ending support, encouragement, and editorial assistance throughout the preparation of this book.

Ronald W. Warwick
Somerset, 1998

QE2

CHAPTER ONE

The British and North American Royal Mail Steam Packet Company

The maritime heritage that gave birth to the *Queen Elizabeth 2* stretches back over a period of nearly a century and a half and involves a transatlantic experience from its inception. The men who conceived the spanning of the western ocean with a line of steamships came together from North America and Great Britain and began 150 years of international cooperation and strong commercial ties sustained by the Cunard Line and the other great North Atlantic lines.

The Industrial Revolution had progressed far enough by the 1830s to make the idea of regular transatlantic communication by means of a fleet of steamships plausible. The desire for a dependable delivery of the mails on which imperial communication and commerce depended prompted the government of Her Majesty Queen Victoria to invite interested parties to tender for a contract. Samuel Cunard of Halifax, Nova Scotia, was the successful contender. His contract to deliver the mails across the Atlantic from Great Britain to North America was signed on May 4, 1839.

Cunard was a highly successful and enterprising Canadian businessman of German ancestry and one of a group of twelve individuals who substantially directed the affairs of Nova Scotia. Largely unknown in Britain, he was the agent of the East India Company in Halifax, and he had been instrumental in establishing a thriving mail service between Halifax, Boston, and Bermuda. He also was one of the founders of the Quebec and Halifax Steam Navigation Company. Their steamer *Royal William* had enjoyed one of the earliest successful crossings of the Atlantic in 1833. Cunard had a reputation for being not only a very astute businessman but also an individual endowed with ex-

Samuel Cunard (1787–1865), of Halifax, Nova Scotia, was the guiding force in 1840 behind the creation of the British and North American Royal Mail Steam Packet Company, which from the very beginning was known as the Cunard Line.

ceptional diplomatic ability. He would need all the ability and charm he possessed to succeed.

In Halifax Cunard's breadth of vision in wanting to tender for the admiralty contract went unappreciated. The reputation of the North Atlantic was too awesome and the steamship, as a mechanical contrivance, too novel for enough of his worthy associates to back him. Accordingly, in January 1839 Cunard sailed for Britain to pursue matters on his own. His willingness to cross the North Atlantic in a sailing ship in midwinter demonstrated the intensity of his ambitions. He carried with him a letter of introduction from the governor general of Nova Scotia, which may have helped him to gain an interview with Charles Wood, the secretary to the admiralty. Wood encouraged the Canadian entrepreneur to submit a formal bid.

The Cunard bid for the privilege of carrying the mails was handed to the admiralty on February 11, 1839, and involved a commitment to provide three steamships of 800 tons and 300 horsepower each. A feeder service from Halifax to Quebec using a smaller vessel was envisaged, as well as another from Halifax to Boston, with the Canadian port being the western terminus of the North Atlantic service. Cunard felt that the contract should run for ten years at a compensation of £55,000 per year. The commitment on the part of Cunard was daring, because at the time of submitting the bid he had neither financial backers for the line nor a builder for the ships.

James C. Melvill, the secretary of the East India Company in London, advised Cunard about who would be the best builder of the new ships. He recommended Robert Napier, of the Scottish firm of Wood & Napier, who had built a number of steamships, including the successful *Berenice* for the East India Company. John Wood built the hulls while Robert Napier was the engineering genius responsible for creating the engines. Napier and Cunard became business associates and close friends; their relationship lasted for the rest of their lives. After Cunard's death in 1869, Napier commissioned a portrait of his friend to be given to Cunard's daughter Elizabeth. In acknowledging receipt of the painting, Elizabeth Cunard thanked Napier "for a gift that must be valuable to me for its own sake, as well as for the sake of the donor, whose name has been familiar to me from early childhood in connection with much I have heard of science and natural energy and talent."*

Cunard wrote to Napier for prices on the ships, and Napier quoted a price of £40 a ton. When Cunard met Napier in Glasgow, he admitted that the quotation was fair, but because he was ordering three identical vessels, he was willing to pay £30,000 per ship for the multiple contract. Napier agreed and Cunard got his ships for £37 a ton—a good Scottish bargain. What Samuel Cunard may not have known was that Napier had developed his own ideas for a transatlantic service as early as 1833 and had drawn plans for vessels of approximately the same size and power as the future Cunarders, but he had not been able to interest anyone in his proposals. At that time the idea of establishing a transatlantic steamship line had seemed as unreasonable as a flight to the moon. Less than a decade later the ships were being ordered.

Robert Napier fully realized that the success of the Cunard ships would be vested in their dependability. If they could depart and arrive on schedule time after time, the public would patronize the vessels and they would earn their keep. Nothing else really mattered. Napier believed that the finest area of the world in which to observe steamship traffic during the late 1830s was the Clyde and the highly competitive short sea route from Glasgow to Belfast. Accordingly, Napier became a familiar figure crossing back and forth on existing steamships, recording their characteristics and evaluating their performances. Out of these observations Napier concluded that the ships Samuel Cunard had ordered were too small and underpowered for dependable service on the North Atlantic. He took the figures to Cunard and the decision was reached to increase the size of the first ships from 800 to 960 tons, and their engines from 300 to 375 horsepower. Unfortunately, the increase in size and horsepower added £2,000 per ship to the cost. In addition, Napier convinced Cunard that at least four ships were needed if year-round operations were to be maintained. The new expense was a hard blow to Cunard's plans, but Napier introduced him to three other Scots, James Donaldson, George Burns, and David MacIver, all of whom had important maritime interests on the Clyde and in Liverpool and were willing to follow where Napier led. The result was the creation of the British and North American Royal Mail Steam

*Cunard Line, *The Cunarders 1840–1969, A Transatlantic Story Spanning 129 Years* (London, 1969), 31.

The first Cunarder built for the North Atlantic was the wooden paddle steamer *Britannia,* which took the first regular sailing of the line from Liverpool to Boston via Halifax on July 4, 1840. Later, during the severe winter of 1840–1841, Boston Harbor froze over, and the local merchants raised a fund to cut a path through the ice to the sea for the *Britannia.*

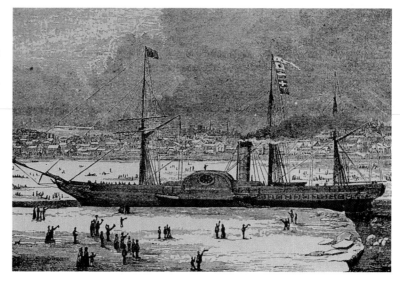

Packet Company, which was founded with a capital of £270,000 acquired in a matter of days from thirty-two businessmen. George Burns's business acumen and good sense were so well known that he became the critical fund raiser, but Samuel Cunard put up the largest amount (£55,000), and the new line was familiarly known as the "Cunard Line" from its inception. The contract for the new ships was signed on March 18, 1839, and now the creation of the enterprise was guaranteed.

One of the strengths of the company from its founding was sufficient capital to establish itself and to weather adversity. Its solid foundation permitted Napier to enlarge the size of the units once again to 1,100 tons and 420 horsepower. At the same time Cunard returned to the admiralty with the information on the ships and suggested that it would be an excellent postal and economic proposition if the vessels continued on to Boston from Halifax. A new contract was signed on July 4, 1839, with an increased subsidy of £60,000 for the enhanced service. The admiralty agreed to Cunard having a biweekly service between March and October and only a monthly service in the winter months of November to February, when the cost in men and ships with little cargo or passengers would be too high. Napier's company was feverishly at work on the engines but he had elected to subcontract for the hulls and the first of these was launched by Robert Duncan of Greenock on February 5, 1840, as *Britannia.*

The mail contract was supposed to take effect on June 4, 1840 but the fitting out and trials of the *Britannia* took a little longer than expected, and she was not ready to sail until July 4, 1840. A special admiralty dispensation was allowed, fortunately, since the penalty for missing a sailing was the very substantial sum of £15,000, one-fourth the annual subsidy. Under normal cir-

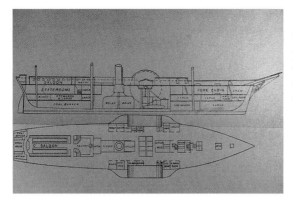

The deck plans of the *Britannia* show the basic arrangement of a paddle steamer, with the machinery and paddle boxes occupying the center of the ship and the passenger areas fore and aft. The 1,135-ton ship, with a length of 207 feet and a breadth of 34 feet, could steam at 9 knots and transport 115 passengers and 225 tons of cargo.

cumstances an unexcused delay in sailing of more than twelve hours resulted in a £500 forfeiture, although the admiralty usually looked with a generous eye upon any mechanical failure or meteorological catastrophe.

The maiden sailing of the *Britannia* captured the imagination of the Liverpool public and she was given a rousing send-off, as commemorated by the famous painting of the occasion. At the time of her commissioning *Britannia* was 1,135 tons, 207 feet in length, and 34 feet in breadth, with a service speed of 9 knots and accommodation for 115 individuals as well as 225 tons of cargo. The *Britannia*, under the command of Commander Henry Woodruff, R.N., sailed with 63 passengers, including Samuel Cunard, and made the 2,534-mile crossing to Halifax in twelve days, ten hours. She remained there a brief eight hours before continuing on to Boston, which she reached in forty-six hours with a net steaming time of fourteen days, eight hours from Liverpool. During the crossing, the engineers had to carefully monitor the consumption of coal to ensure that there would be enough left to reach to reach Halifax or Boston. Coal was like gold to the new steamship line, costing 8 shillings ($10.00)* a ton in Liverpool and 20 shillings ($25.00) a ton in Boston. The projections were made that the furnaces would consume 9,960 tons of coal a year.

The citizens of Boston gave the ship and her owner a hero's welcome. Contemporary accounts credit Samuel Cunard with receiving 1,873 invitations to dinner from delighted Bostonians. He was presented with a large ornate silver vase suitably engraved with a commemorative inscription and a picture of the *Britannia*, which is now on display in a showcase by the entrance to the Yacht Club on the *Queen Elizabeth 2*.

The *Unicorn*, a 640-ton paddle steamer hitherto of the Burns line, made her maiden voyage between Glasgow and Liverpool on May 16, 1840—three

---

* Throughout the text the monetary exchange rate is that of the year concerned.

months before the *Britannia*. The *Unicorn* established the feeder service between Pictou and Quebec, although on the first crossing she continued from Halifax to Boston with Cunard Line supplies. The *Britannia*'s own return crossing to Liverpool from Boston took only ten days with the Gulf Stream and favorable winds to help. More often than not, most eastbound crossings were faster than westbound ones. Subsequently the *Britannia* was followed by the *Arcadia*, the *Caledonia*, and the *Columbia*, with the last of the four being in operation by January 5, 1841.

The Cunard Line quoted the one-class fares at 34 guineas (£35.7, or $882.40) to Halifax and 38 guineas to Boston, initially with all food and wine included. After about nine months it was stated in the company literature that all wines and liquor would be extra. Costs soon outran all estimates and the situation became quite serious. The partners put together a forthright explanation of their position for the admiralty, and, after due consideration, the subsidy was raised to £81,000 per year, but with the understanding that a fifth steamer would be built to insure the continuity of service in the case of disaster. The *Hibernia* entered service on April 18, 1843, and proved herself a record breaker with a crossing from Halifax to Liverpool in nine days, ten hours at 11.21 knots. The wisdom of the admiralty's insistence on a fifth vessel soon was made dramatically clear when the *Columbia* was wrecked in dense fog on Seal Island near Cape Sable. All passengers and crew were rescued and transported to Halifax and Liverpool by the *Margaret*, a paddle steamer that normally alternated with the *Unicorn* in the Canadian feeder service. The company did not even have to charter a replacement vessel and lose the fares of those who were saved by virtue of this stroke of luck. Cunard also began to establish a reputation for safety that eventually would give them the proud record of not having lost, through the fault of the company, a single passenger at sea during peacetime in nearly 159 years. When news of the disaster to the *Columbia* reached Liverpool a replacement was promptly ordered and named *Cambria*.

Without the Admiralty subsidy all the other British-flag North Atlantic passenger lines ceased to exist by 1846. Cunard was willing to extend operations to New York if an appropriate contract could be negotiated. This was achieved in 1847 when the subsidy for carrying the mails was increased to £156,000 in return for Cunard's commitment to maintain a weekly service during the period March through October and a biweekly sailing during the winter months. The feeder service from Pictou to Quebec never lived up to Cunard expectations and was withdrawn.

The *Hibernia* sailed from New York on January 1, 1848, thereby beginning Cunard's long association with that American port. Four new paddle steamers were ordered to maintain the new schedule and they were substantially larger than the original ships of the fleet, with dimensions of 251 by 38 feet and a passenger capacity of 140. Napier again won the contract for the ships

The great American competitor of Samuel Cunard in the 1850s was Edward Knight Collins (1802–1878), who founded the New York and Liverpool United States' Mail Steam-Ship Company in 1850, which was universally known as the Collins Line.

and built the engines while subcontracting the hulls. The first of the new steamers was the 1,826-ton *America* and her sister ships were the *Niagra*, *Europa*, and *Canada*, all completed in 1848. This brought the Cunard Line up to a fleet of nine ships, six of which were sufficient to maintain the weekly service. Hence the first two ships, the *Britannia* and the *Arcadia*, were sold to the German Confederation Navy. The *Britannia* continued in service until sunk as a target vessel in 1880. Among the new vessels, the *Canada* distinguished herself by an eastward passage of eight days, twelve hours, forty-four minutes from Halifax to Liverpool at an average speed of 12.41 knots.*

The guiding philosophy of the British and North American Steam Packet Company was conservatism. Under no circumstances would the Cunard Line tackle innovations or major advances in marine architecture or propulsion until the results were well established by other steamship lines. Upon occasion this placed the Cunard Line at a disadvantage when superior ships were brought into service by enterprising competitors. However, the Cunard fleet also contained very few unsatisfactory ships during the nineteenth century and their safety record was unmatched by any competitor.

In the 1850s the great opponent of the Cunard Line was an American-flag company, the New York & Liverpool United States' Mail Steam-Ship Company, universally known as the Collins Line after its principal founder, Edward Knight Collins. This American venture was established with the goal of providing a direct service from New York to Liverpool with larger, faster, and more luxurious vessels than Cunard. The first Collins steamers were named

*N.R.P. Bonsor, *North Atlantic Seaway* (Jersey, 1975), vol. 5: 1876.

The *Atlantic* was the first Collins steamer. At 2,845 tons, 284 feet by 50 feet, and 12 knots, she was substantially larger and faster than the Cunard competition. The Collins steamers proved to be record breakers, but also prone to accident, since they were driven hard. The disastrous losses of the *Arctic* in 1854 and the *Pacific* in 1856, when combined with a reduction of the American subsidy, brought the line to an end in 1858.

for the great bodies of water of the world. The 2,845-ton *Atlantic*, followed by the *Pacific*, *Arctic*, and *Baltic*, were substantially larger than even the newest Cunarders (*America* class, 1,826 tons), surpassing them by over 1,000 tons. Collins also was the proud possessor of a United States Post Office mail subsidy of $385,000. When the *Atlantic* made her maiden departure from New York, on April 27, 1850, the American newspapers were generous in their praise, but they had good reason to be. The new liner boasted luxurious private cabins with paneling and damask drapes, a generous-sized dining saloon, steam heat throughout, and a means by which each occupant of a major cabin could communicate with the steward in order to obtain service. The result of such luxury was that the Collins Line soon was garnering for itself the cream of the traffic. In Liverpool one of the local newspapers printed a little ditty to the effect that Cunard should charter the Collins ships to pull the Cunarders over. Unfortunately for E. K. Collins, his ships cost substantially more to build than had been expected and much more to maintain in service than had been projected. The United States Congress took notice of these factors when it agreed to increase the Collins Line subsidy from $385,000 to $858,000 in return for biweekly service all year. An additional stipulation was that the U.S. government could cancel the subsidy at any time on six months' notice. On May 10, 1851, the luxurious *Pacific* sailed from New York and thrashed her way across in the record-breaking time of nine days, twenty hours, fourteen minutes, with 240 passengers. Collins ships were carrying 50 percent more passengers than Cunard. Yet Samuel Cunard had the perspicacity to protect his company's revenues by reaching a working agreement with the Americans. The result was that from May 25, 1850, through March 31, 1855, the vast majority of the income of the two lines was shared on the basis of one third to Collins and two thirds to Cunard, an arrangement that supplied

Collins with a guaranteed income and share of the trade. The two great rivals were certainly among the most friendly of competitors for the better part of five years until Collins became overwhelmed by adversity.*

The Collins Line ships were driven terribly hard, and gangs of workers reportedly swarmed over them whenever they were in New York. Disaster struck on September 27, 1854, when the *Arctic*, nearing Cape Race in dense fog, collided with the French steamer *Vesta*. Extending superhuman effort to reach land, the *Arctic* went down nearly five hours later, taking with her somewhere between 285 and 351 individuals of the 383 on board. Included among those who lost their lives were E. K. Collins's wife, son, and daughter, transforming a business catastrophe into a shattering personal loss.

Cunard was not in a position to take the maximum advantage of this situation, since many of their ships had been chartered by the British government as troop transports because of the Crimean War (1853–1856). It was the first time assistance was rendered to the government by the Cunard Line. Collins was therefore able to continue his business despite the disaster. The final blow came when the *Pacific* sailed from Liverpool on January 23, 1856, and was never heard of again. The presumption has always been that the vessel hit an iceberg and went under without a survivor or trace. To his credit, E. K. Collins chartered a ship, loaded her with supplies, and sent her out to crisscross the North Atlantic, searching steamer lanes without success. Congress gave notice of reducing the subsidy in August 1857 and the ill-fated Collins Line wound up operations in 1858.

The Cunard Line had elected to meet the threat of the Collins Line ships by building the iron paddle steamer *Persia* (1856). The new liner, at 3,300 tons, 376 by 45 feet, and $13\frac{1}{2}$ knots, was built from the keel up to be a record breaker. She was three times the size of the *Britannia*, with engines five times as large that burned twice as much coal. She also could carry more than twice as many passengers in luxury equaling that of the Collins Line vessels. The *Persia* soon captured the transatlantic record with a crossing of nine days, ten hours, twenty-two minutes from New York to Liverpool at 13.47 knots, nearly half a knot faster than the best speed of the Collins paddlers, and regularly improved upon her records. She was the first iron-hulled Cunard mail steamer and marks another major advance in marine technology for the line even if other concerns, such as Royal Mail, had pioneered the use of iron.† Wood had become increasingly unacceptable for oceangoing steam vessels, and for the next forty years British yards were far ahead of all others as regards iron and steel for shipbuilding. In fact, not until the four-funnel *Kaiser*

* Francis E. Hyde, *Cunard and the North Atlantic, 1840–1973* (London, 1975), 39–45.
† N.R.P. Bonsor, *South Atlantic Seaway* (Jersey, 1935), 5.

The paddle steamer *Persia* (1856) was part of the Cunard response to the Collins Line. She was the first iron-hulled mail steamer in the Cunard fleet and marked the critical transition from wood to iron as a building material. This technological advance would make British shipbuilding yards dominant in the world for the next forty years.

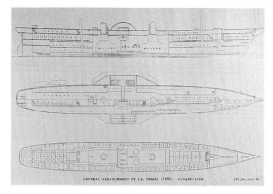

The *Persia* captured the transatlantic record with a crossing of 9 days, 10 hours, 22 minutes from New York to Liverpool at an average speed of 13.47 knots. Last of the Cunard paddle steamers built for the North Atlantic, she was a substantial improvement at 3,300 tons, 376 feet by 45 feet, and 13.5 knots.

Wilhelm der Grosse (1897) was constructed in a German yard for the North German Lloyd Line would there be a non-British built record breaker.*

The Cunard Line broadened out into other fields of commercial activity besides the North Atlantic. In 1853 ships started to run from Liverpool to the Mediterranean, calling at Gibraltar, Malta, and Istanbul. Initially the arrangement was somewhat informal, but as trade developed the British & Foreign Steam Navigation Company was created, with ownership shared by Samuel Cunard, George Burns, and Charles MacIver, who was rapidly becoming the dominant force on the Liverpool maritime scene. In time the Mediterranean trade represented a substantial percentage of the total income Cunard vessels earned, particularly as the immigrant trade from southern Europe increased after the American Civil War (1861–1865). Between 1858 and 1861 seven sister ships of around 1,800 tons were constructed for the Mediterranean trade (*Palestine, Olympus, Marathon, Atlas, Hecla, Kedar, Sidon,* and *Morocco*), while five more vessels (*Tarifa, Tripoli, Aleppo, Malta,* and *Palmyra*) of 2,000 tons followed in their wake between 1861 and 1863. Periodically all these ships, except the *Morocco*, took North Atlantic sailings when trading conditions or need warranted. They all carried a relatively small number of "cabin class" passengers (40–70) but had generous steerage accommodations for 500 or more. The *Sidon* carried in excess of 300 steerage class

---

* John H. Shaum, Jr., and William H. Flayhart III, *Majesty at Sea, The Four Stackers* (New York, 1981), 9.

George Burns (1795–1890) was a Scotsman with shipping interests on both the Clyde and Mersey. When Samuel Cunard needed additional capital to finance the first ships, Robert Napier introduced him to George Burns, who was able to persuade a substantial number of investors to follow his lead.

Charles MacIver (1811–1885) was a very astute and unrelenting Liverpool shipowner who became a major force in the Cunard Line. In 1878, MacIver was the senior godfather at the birth of the Cunard Steam-Ship Company Limited when the existing partners turned the firm public in order to raise money for new tonnage.

passengers to New York from Liverpool and Queenstown (Cóbh, Ireland) in May 1863, and subsequently much greater numbers were common.

Cunard commissioned two outstanding ships in 1862. One, the 3,871-ton paddle steamer *Scotia*, represented the end of an era since she was the last major ship in the fleet to use paddles for propulsion; the other, the 2,638-ton *China*, was the first Cunard-built mail steamer to be driven by propellers. Cunard had been a little slow in recognizing the superiority of propellers over paddles for first-class tonnage, but by the mid-1860s there remained little doubt about the matter. The huge machinery of the paddlers occupied the prime commercial area of the ship amidships and they required enormous quantities of coal. A propeller-driven vessel was much more economical to run and permitted the positioning of the very best and most expensive cabins in the center section of the ship. Furthermore, there was little room left for steerage in a paddle-driven mail steamer, and the immigrant trade could not be ignored. The *China*, of 2,638 tons, consumed 80 tons of coal a day at 12 knots; whereas the *Scotia*, of 3,871, burned 160 tons to produce 14 knots. As a return on investment the *China* could carry 268 cabin and 771 steerage class passengers as well as an additional 1,400 tons of cargo. In contrast, the *Scotia* had accommodation for 573 cabin and no steerage passengers and carried only 1,050 tons of cargo. The great thrashing paddles of the *Scotia* may have inspired confidence and been impressive, but the slim, screw-propelled hull of the *China* spelled profits in the Cunard ledgers.

The financial success of the *China* inspired the Cunard Line to order additional vessels, including the *Russia* (1867), which was the first screw Cunarder to equal the size and speed of the first-class paddlers. The *Russia* joined the *Scotia* and the *Persia* in the biweekly service between Liverpool and New York. This combination provided travelers with an interesting opportunity to evaluate paddles versus screws in relatively equal vessels as part of the premier service of a great North Atlantic line.

The official Cunard mail connection with Boston came to an end in 1867, when the new mail contract, now drawn up by the postmaster general instead of the admiralty, assigned to Cunard the responsibility for weekly service from Liverpool via Queenstown to New York in return for a subsidy of £80,000. The Inman Line, a Cunard rival, secured the mail contract for the Liverpool-Boston route, but Cunard did not abandon the port that had treated them so generously. Biweekly service was initiated with secondary steamers in 1867 and revised upward to weekly service in the following year.

Sir Samuel Cunard had been honored by Queen Victoria with a baronetcy in 1858 for his contributions to trade and commerce and for the service rendered by the ships of his line to the British cause in the Crimean War and the Sepoy (Indian) Mutiny (1857), when many ships were used as troop transports and supply vessels. The twenty-fifth anniversary year of the Cunard Line in 1865 brought cause for celebration and cause for sadness. The same newspaper carrying the news of the assassination of President Abraham Lincoln ran the obituary of Samuel Cunard, who died on April 28, 1865, at the age of seventy-eight. David MacIver died in 1845, to be succeeded by his energetic brother Charles. George Burns retired in 1860, although he lived to the advanced age of ninety-five, while Robert Napier reached eighty-six.

The two decades between the 1850s and the 1870s saw the creation of a number of formidable rivals of the Cunard Line. In Britain were founded the Inman Line (1850), Anchor Line (1856), Guion Line (1863), and White Star Line (1871). On the continent, the Hamburg-American Line started a steamship service in 1856, followed by the aforementioned North German

Lloyd Line (1858), Compagnie Generale Transatlantique (French Line, 1864), the Red Star Line, and Holland-America (1873), in the United States the American Line (1873), and in Italy the Navigazione Generale Italiana (1881).

None of these companies affected the future of the Cunard Line as much as the founding of the White Star Line. Cunard had lost the Blue Riband to the Inman Line in 1869 after holding it for thirteen years. However, the White Star Line inaugurated a service in 1871 between Liverpool and New York with a fleet of ships having compound engines and passenger accommodations so far ahead of existing standards that they outdated the entire Cunard fleet overnight. Cunard did all they reasonably could in the way of modernizing their existing ships. The *Hecla, Olympus, Marathon,* and *Atlas* were lengthened by 60 feet, thereby increasing their tonnage to 2,400, and the other ships were fitted with compound engines. Much more important was the commissioning of the 4,550-ton *Bothnia* in 1874 and *Sythia* in 1875. They were larger but slower than the White Star liner *Oceanic* (1871).[*]

In due course the Cunard owners decided that, in the face of the White Star competition, there was no alternative but to establish a public company. In 1878 the assets of the founders, or their heirs, in the British and North American Royal Mail Steam Packet Company and in the British & Foreign Steam Navigation Company were transferred to the new Cunard Steam-Ship Company Limited. The partners received stock worth a total of £1,200,000 out of the £2,000,000 and two years later a general offering was made to the British public of the remaining £800,000, which was subscribed immediately. The Cunard prospectus simply stated: "The growing wants of the Company's transatlantic trade demand the acquisition of additional steam ships of great size and power, involving a cost for construction which may best be met by a large public company."[†]

The new influx of capital made it possible in 1881 to order the first steel Cunarder, the 7,392-ton *Servia.* The *Servia* attracted considerable attention when she entered service on November 26, 1881, and received many favorable comments about the luxury of her first-class accommodations for 480 in the first class and 750 in steerage, which was critical to any steamship line's success. The *Servia* was an outstanding Cunard ship but she only followed existing trends. Other liners before her had been built of steel (*Buenos Ayrean,* and *Parisian* of the Allan Line), or were larger (*City of Rome,* 8,415 tons, of the Inman Line), or were faster (*Arizona,* Guion Line). In the luxury of her accommodations the *Servia* approached the ships of the White Star Line, Cu-

[*]Bonsor, *North Atlantic Seaway.*
[†]Cunard Line, *The Cunarders 1840–1969.*

nard's closest competitor, and began to lure back some of the traveling public Cunard had lost in previous years.

The completion of the *Aurania* (1883) reinforced the first-class fleet, but this ship certainly experienced some teething troubles. Outward bound to New York on her maiden voyage the *Aurania*'s engines blew up in mid-Atlantic. Once again, with phenomenal good luck, there was no loss of life. She completed her crossing under sail, ultimately making her maiden arrival in New York Harbor eleven days out from Liverpool with the assistance of three tugs. The damage to her engines was so severe that she was dispatched to Glasgow using only a low-pressure cylinder and did not return to service for nearly a year. After repairs were made, however, she proved herself a worthy addition to the fleet and provided dependable sailings for the next fifteen years.

Cunard occasionally acquired a vessel through luck; this was the case in 1884 when the Guion Line was in severe financial difficulties as a direct result of the trade depression and could not make the payments to the builders for their new *Oregon*. Cunard bought the vessel and she took her maiden sailing for the line on June 8, 1884. The 7,375-ton *Oregon* was constructed of iron and she was again to prove herself a record breaker as she romped outward bound to New York in six days, nine hours, forty-two minutes (18.16 knots) on her third Cunard crossing and home to Liverpool in six days, eleven hours, nine minutes at an average speed of 18.39 knots. The result for Cunard was a record-breaking passenger liner for the first time in fifteen years.

War scares in the mid-1880s periodically occurred all around the British Empire, from the Balkans to the Middle East, Africa, Northern India, and the Far East. Although no major conflict occurred until World War I, the fact that war clouds often looked so ominous was reason for the admiralty to charter Cunard vessels, even if on a temporary basis. The *Oregon* was required for admiralty service in 1885 as an armed merchant cruiser. When she was returned to Cunard, she commenced a new express service to Boston. The *Oregon* sailed from Liverpool with nearly 900 on her last scheduled voyage to New York.

Cunard's safety record over its entire history is little short of phenomenal, because not a single passenger's life has been lost through the company's fault at sea during peacetime. Upon occasions they have been very lucky. The *Malta* (1866, 2,132 tons) of the Mediterranean service was lost in a spectacular wreck near Land's End on October 10, 1889, without loss of life.

The *Oregon* (7,374 tons, 501 feet by 54.2 feet, 18 knots) was acquired in 1884. The *Oregon* obtained the Blue Riband of the Atlantic for Cunard in August 1884. On March 14, 1886, the liner was in a collision with an unknown sailing vessel eighteen miles east of Long Island, N.Y., and sank. All passengers and crew were rescued by the North German Lloyd liner *Fulda*.

Approaching Long Island on March 14, 1886, she collided with an unknown sailing ship. The two vessels parted in the fog and the *Oregon* rapidly began to sink. Fortunately, the North German Lloyd steamer *Fulda* was nearby. She rescued all the passengers and crew of the *Oregon*, thus preserving the distinguished reputation of the Cunard Line.

The loss of the *Oregon* was deeply regretted, but Cunard still had adequate tonnage available. The delivery of the 7,718-ton *Umbria* and *Etruria* in November 1884 and April 1885, respectively, gave them a well-balanced first-class fleet again. Both ships were record breakers and they were the last large greyhounds to have compound engines and only a single propeller. An interesting feature of both ships was that they improved in their performance with the passage of time. The premier Cunard service from Liverpool to New York was maintained by the excellent quartet of the *Servia, Aurania, Umbria*, and *Etruria* after 1885. This would have been adequate for the next ten years under normal conditions of ship renewal; however, this was not to be the case. Competition on the North Atlantic went wild with the building of new ocean greyhounds, and patrons of the various steamship lines plying these sea lanes sometimes referred to it as the "frantic Atlantic."

In the mid-1880s the severe economic depression that drove the Guion Line into bankruptcy also threatened the financial stability of the Inman Line, whose founder, William Inman, had died in 1881. Shortly thereafter the Inman Line had taken delivery of the *City of Rome*, arguably one of the most beautiful ships ever to cross the Atlantic. Unfortunately, the *City of Rome*, which had been contracted for as a steel-hulled vessel, had been built of iron because of a shortage of the other metal. As a result, she was both slower and carried fewer passengers than had been anticipated. The Inman Line, in the uncertainty following William Inman's death, returned the ship to the builders and refused to accept her. The fortunes of the line deteriorated sub-

The publications of steamship lines provide a valuable description of their services. In 1897, Cunard was operating a fleet of twenty-four vessels in addition to other tonnage chartered when needed.

stantially in the economic depression of the next four years and their ships fell far behind those of Cunard and White Star, the other Liverpool shipping giants. Some discussion took place between T. H. Ismay of White Star and other Liverpool shipowners about saving the Inman Line. Ismay reportedly was ready to lend as much as £1,000,000 to the bankrupt company, but Cunard and others were unwilling.* The idea behind Ismay's charity was "never to let a weak man out of your trade, thus letting a strong one in," a doctrine verified when Clement Griscom, the Philadelphia shipping magnate, succeeded in gaining control of the Inman Line and the concern was reborn as the Inman & International Steamship Company Ltd. (1886). The rejuvenated steamship line went to its builders for two greatly improved vessels, *City of New York* (1888) and *City of Paris* (1889), which in turn forced Cunard and White Star to build in response when neither really wanted to have the expense. In the long run it probably would have been far less a strain to have kept the Inman Line in operation.

Cunard immediately retaliated against the new American owners of the Inman Line by insisting that they would have nothing to do with any postal contract involving that line. Critical discussions ensued during which Cunard was even warned it might be sued for failing to carry the mails, but the line held firm and was supported by White Star. The subsequent mail contract called for a reduction of the official sailings from Liverpool from three a week

*Roy Anderson, *White Star* (Lancashire, 1964), 87.

The Cunard Passenger Log Book for 1897 is graced with a drawing of the *Campania* (1893, 12,950 tons), which, with her sister ship, *Lucania* (1893, 12,952 tons), and the *Umbria* (1884, 7,718 tons) and *Etruria* (1885, 7,718 tons), maintained the first-class North Atlantic service. These ships were capable of regular crossings at 19 to 21 knots, and the *Campania* and *Lucania* were among the fastest Atlantic liners from 1893 to 1897.

to twice weekly, with the Tuesday Inman sailing eliminated. The refusal to share the postal revenues in some ways backfired: It led to the creation of the rejuvenated American Line of 1893 and, ultimately, to John Pierpont Morgan's huge American shipping trust, the International Mercantile Marine, in 1902.

The new ships ordered by the American Line forced Cunard and the other major shipping lines back to their builders for new tonnage. The result for Cunard was the commissioning of the 12,950-ton twin-screw *Campania* and *Lucania* in 1893. These famous ships were propelled by twin sets of five-cylinder, triple-expansion engines, which were so large that their engine rooms were virtual cathedrals of the Industrial Revolution. They were the first Cunarders to dispense with sails as a safety measure. The *Campania* and *Lucania* were designed to take all the luxury of a wealthy Victorian home to sea. Solid paneling, heavy brocade, rich wood carvings, stained glass windows, and palm

The *Carmania* (1905, 19,524 tons), a large intermediate liner built for the Cunard Line, was outfitted with the "new" steam turbines as a working experiment. Her sister ship, *Caronia* (1905, 19,687 tons), was given quadruple-expansion engines. The result was that the *Carmania* was $^3/_4$ knot faster, or slightly cheaper to operate at the same speed. Accordingly, the decision was made to equip the two new giant Cunarders with turbines.

The Cunard Liner "CARMANIA"

The *Ivernia* and *Saxonia* (1900, 14,058 and 14,281 tons, respectively) were two large intermediate liners created for the Liverpool–Boston service. Liverpool was the Cunard European terminus; but the tide conditions in the Mersey made it difficult for larger ships to come alongside the pier on many occasions.

Landing Stage from the Mersey, Liverpool.

trees were all part of the decor. These impressive ships were very popular with the wealthy traveling public. Cunard Line brochures of the 1890s stressed the fact that the *Campania* and *Lucania* could provide the ultimate luxury of "privacy" for the single person in that they were fitted with a number of single-berth cabins. In earlier ships, even in first class, a single passenger frequently had to share a cabin with another traveler. Most travelers still expected to share facilities, but at least the option of complete privacy was available, at an appropriate surcharge. Another first for Cunard was the provision of suites consisting of a single or double cabin with an adjoining sitting room. The popularity of the "Suites" among the wealthiest clientele made them a planned part of future tonnage.

The *Campania* and *Lucania* proved themselves fast and solid performers. The *Campania* was responsible for the fastest maiden voyage on record, in

The *Carpathia* (1903, 13,555 tons) carried cargo, 204 second-class, and 1,500 third-class passengers. She was employed extensively in the immigrant trade between Trieste on the Adriatic and New York. On the night of April 12, 1912, the *Carpathia* was outward bound from New York to the Mediterranean when she heard the distress signal of the giant White Star liner *Titanic* and went to her aid. All of the 700 survivors were rescued by her.

April 1893, and for regaining the eastbound Blue Riband for the Cunard Line by sailing home in five days, seventeen hours, twenty-seven minutes at an average speed of 21.30 knots, followed by a record 21.12 knots westbound. The two ships were well balanced and frequently averaged over 21 knots both westbound and eastbound for many successive voyages. Of the two ships the *Lucania* was slightly faster. Such dependability earned the respect of the public and brought dividends, although the competition between Cunard and White Star in Liverpool and the American Line ships sailing from Southampton was cutthroat. Furthermore, the challenge of the continental lines such as the German HAPAG, North German Lloyd, and the Compagnie Generale Transatlantique was becoming increasingly acute. Cunard was impressed by the competition, but the firm's first priority was to make a profit, not record breakers. The latter were exceedingly costly to build, maintain, and operate, rarely making money unless they were integrated into a carefully developed fleet program.

The premier new ships of the Cunard fleet at the turn of the century were the 14,000-ton *Ivernia* and *Saxonia,* specifically designed for the Liverpool to Boston trade, where they proved themselves to be among the most popular ships in any fleet on the North Atlantic. At 15 knots no speed record was threatened, but the *Ivernia* and *Saxonia,* sporting the tallest single funnels ever given a North Atlantic steamer (106 feet), had accommodations in three classes for 1,964 passengers. On April 23, 1901, when a large number of small children and infants were being carried, the *Saxonia* sailed from Liverpool with the astonishing number of 2,260 souls on the passenger list. She and the *Ivernia* were among the most profitable single ships in the Cunard fleet.

The creation of J. P. Morgan's International Mercantile Marine Corporation in the period 1901–1903 placed a premium on the Cunard Line remaining

The *Lusitania* (1907, 31,550 tons) remains one of the most famous of all Cunarders. She was the first of the giant trio built by the line between 1907 and 1914 to maintain the first-class service. A highly successful vessel with an average speed of 23.99 knots, she captured the Blue Riband in October 1907. After eight years of commercial service she was torpedoed on May 7, 1915, off the Irish coast and went down with 1,198 souls in twenty minutes.

British. The White Star Line and numerous other concerns either were bought by the IMM or signed agreements with the shipping trust. Even Albert Ballin, HAPAG, agreed to reduce competition with J. P. Morgan. Cunard felt the pressure acutely and approached the British government with the proposition that the line would build two new contestants for the Atlantic record and remain both a British-flag and British-owned company if the government would extend assistance in financing the needed tonnage. The alternative was the selling out of the last major British steamship line on the North Atlantic to foreign ownership. After a considerable period of hard negotiating the British government agreed to assist the Cunard Line with the necessary financing of the proposed superships provided they remained British in every way and available to the admiralty whenever needed.

Having arranged financing, Cunard's next major problem was the character of the propulsion system for new ships. Should they involve the traditional reciprocating engines or the still-novel Parsons turbines? The decision was made to experiment in two similar ships with the different propulsion systems. Two large intermediate steamers, the *Carmania* and the *Caronia* (20,000 tons), were ordered for delivery in 1905. The *Carmania* was constructed with the new steam turbines and proved herself to be appreciably faster and somewhat less expensive to run. As a result Cunard became daring in the conception of its fleet for the first time since Samuel Cunard ordered the initial quartet and decided to build two giant liners powered with the largest turbines then available. Technology was to be stretched to the limits in the creation of these ships. The contract for one of the liners was won by John Brown on the Clyde, and the other went to Swan, Hunter & Wigham Richardson on the Tyne.

June 7, 1906, marked a milestone not only in the history of the Cunard Line but also in the entire development of the transatlantic ferry. On that day John

Cunard R.M.S. "MAURETANIA" (Turbine).
THE LARGEST VESSEL IN THE WORLD.
32,600 Tons ; 68,000 H.P. ; Service speed 25 Knots
Length 787 ft. ; Breadth 88 ft. ; Depth 60½ ft.

The *Mauretania* (1907, 31,938 tons) was the second of the Cunard big three before World War I. Entering service two months after the *Lusitania*, she proved herself slightly faster and held the Blue Riband from 1907 to 1929. A consistent performer between 1909 and 1911, she averaged well over 25 knots for forty-four round-trip voyages.

Brown launched the *Lusitania* and instantaneously all the first-class tonnage on the North Atlantic became obsolete. The *Lusitania* was the largest ship in the world at 31,550 tons with a length of 762 feet and a breadth of 88 feet. She had accommodation for 563 in first, 464 in second, and 1,138 in third class, and sailed at capacity on her maiden voyage, on September 7, 1907. Superlatives greeted her wherever she went and she totally fulfilled the expectations of her owners and builders by making the fastest crossing of the Atlantic in both directions during October 1907 at speeds of 23.99 knots westbound and 23.61 knots eastbound. The *Lusitania* thus became the first ship to take the Atlantic crossing in less than five days, even if only by fractions and from Queenstown. The *Mauretania* followed after some adjustments for vibration and soon proved herself a worthy consort to her sister. The two ships exchanged the Blue Riband back and forth for nearly two years, until the installation of new propellers on the *Mauretania* gave her the advantage over the *Lusitania*. With a record passage of four days, ten hours, fifty-one minutes at an average speed of 26.06 knots over a distance of 2,784 miles from Queenstown to New York, the *Mauretania* created a record that stood for twenty years. If the *Lusitania* was "the" ship as the first of the new class of superliners, the *Mauretania* became one of the most popular and beloved ships ever to grace the North Atlantic during a full career from 1907 to 1935.

The loss of the aging *Lucania* to fire in the Huskisson Dock, Liverpool, during August 1909 underlined the need for a third vessel to partner the big two. Accordingly, Cunard ordered a slightly larger but slower version of their two speed queens, thus creating the *Aquitania*. She was one of the largest ships in the world, at 45,647 tons, when delivered in 1914. Basically she was *Lusitania* with an extra deck but with a standard of appointments that made her one of the most distinguished ships of her era. Her speed of 23 knots made it possible to deliver her 3,263 passengers to New York in a balanced three-ship sched-

The *Aquitania* (1914, 45,647 tons) was the third of the giant Cunarders before World War I. Basically a *Lusitania* with an additional deck, the *Aquitania* was the epitome of luxury, even if slightly slower, at 23 knots, than her consorts. She fitted into the three-ship service beautifully and survived to serve in both world wars, being scrapped only in 1950.

ule with the *Lusitania* and *Mauretania*. The basic idea was to have one ship ready to sail from Liverpool, one ready to sail from New York, and one in mid-Atlantic, thereby maintaining the weekly sailing schedule from both sides of the Atlantic.

The *Aquitania* barely had time to complete three voyages in 1914 before the beginning of World War I plunged Britain into the first general European war in ninety-nine years. She was requisitioned for duty as an armed merchant cruiser, but this service was short-lived because her size made her too vulnerable. Furthermore, on August 25, 1914, the *Aquitania* returned to Liverpool with heavy damage to her bow as the result of a collision with the Leyland liner *Canadian* off the coast of Ireland. Shortly afterward, the *Mauretania* joined the *Aquitania* in lay-up until satisfactory employment for these valuable ships could be found.

The *Lusitania* maintained a reduced Cunard sailing schedule by herself for the first few months of 1915. Her last sailing from New York, under the command of Captain W. T. Turner, commenced on May 1, 1915, with 1,959 passengers and crew onboard. Five days later, as the big Cunarder approached the Irish Coast near the Old Head of Kinsale, she was torpedoed by the German submarine U-20 and went down with 1,198 of those who had sailed with her. The subsequent international furor over unrestricted submarine warfare contributed to the American decision to enter World War I on the side of the Allies in April 1917 after Germany resumed such activity.

In May 1915 the *Mauretania* and the *Aquitania* were converted into troopships for use in the Mediterranean in support of the Dardanelles Campaign. Following their trooping duties both ships also served for a period as hospital ships painted white with great red crosses emblazoned on their sides and sporting buff funnels. Subsequently the ships served as troopships for the Canadian forces bound to Europe and then, after April 1917, for the American Expeditionary Force as it crossed to France. Immediately following the armistice the steamship lines were desperate for tonnage and as quickly as possible the *Mauretania* and *Aquitania* were returned to Cunard to handle the flood of travelers trying to cross the Atlantic. It was decided that they would partially replace the prewar German lines in the Southampton–Cherbourg–New York trade, the first such sailing being taken by the *Aquitania* on June 14, 1919. Both ships required extensive renovation of all passenger accommodation and a total overhaul of their machinery after the rigors of wartime service. The decision was made to convert both ships from coal to oil, which would eliminate the horrendous labor of coaling the giant liners in port and of maintaining the coal-fired boilers at sea. In fact, the crews of the ships were reduced from 350 to 50 in the "stokers" category.

The loss of the *Lusitania* might have made Cunard short of first-class tonnage for the three-ship service if it had not been possible to acquire the ex-HAPAG liner *Imperator* (1913), which was renamed the *Berengaria*. The *Imperator* and her sister ship, *Bismarck,* were both assigned as war reparations to Britain after World War I and were bought by Cunard and White Star jointly in order to avoid outbidding each other. This cooperative effort remained in force for approximately ten years, although each line assumed

The *Berengaria* (1920, 52,226 tons, 22 knots) was launched as the HAPAG *Imperator* in 1912. After the war she became the Cunard *Berengaria*, named for the wife of Richard I, the "lion hearted." As such she was the largest Cunarder and replaced the lost *Lusitania* in the weekly express service.

The second *Mauretania* (1938–1965) was generally regarded as a smaller version of the *Queen Elizabeth*. Like her predecessor, she was used by the British government as a troopship. After the war was over, she was employed on the Atlantic trade in the summer months, carrying 1,360 passengers in three classes of accommodation. During the winter she cruised to the West Indies, and the passenger carry was restricted to 750 in one class. In 1962, the hull of the ship was painted pale green, and from then on she was employed mainly in cruising. She remained in service until being sold to Scottish breakers in 1965.

complete control of its own vessel. White Star renamed their ship the *Majestic*, but she only had one suitable running mate, the *Olympic*. Cunard therefore had the best-balanced trio of giant ships on the Atlantic from 1919 to 1935 with the *Mauretania*, *Aquitania*, and *Berengaria*.

The 1920s saw Cunard rebuilding its fleet but with great caution because the revision of the American immigration laws all but eliminated the need for steerage. In place of the immigrant trade came an ever-increasing group of American tourists. Parts of the third-class quarters were modified and up-graded as tourist third cabin (later shortened to tourist class) in recognition of the increase. The 1920s were not a boom time everywhere, and competition on the North Atlantic for travelers was fierce. As a result, much wider use of vessels for cruising came into vogue, particularly during the winter months. By the late 1920s the introduction of new first-class tonnage by German and Italian lines emphasized the need for Cunard to prepare the plans for the next generation of superliners. When White Star ordered a 60,000-ton ship and the French Line signed a contract for an 80,000-ton vessel, time became criti-cal. Insofar as Cunard was concerned the ultimate North Atlantic service ap-peared obtainable.

Samuel Cunard in 1840 had built a fleet of four ships in order to ensure reg-ular service across the Atlantic. Initially biweekly, the service soon was estab-lished on a weekly basis, with ships sailing from either side of the Atlantic on a given day each week. Throughout the intervening ninety years every major advance in marine technology had resulted in larger, faster, and fewer ships to maintain the first-class service. By 1893 the *Umbria, Etruria, Campania,* and *Lucania* were capable of maintaining Cunard's weekly sailings. By 1907 it was possible for Cunard to think in terms of three ships for the first-class service from Britain to the United States, and the *Lusitania, Mauretania,* and *Aquitania* had been born. Now in the late 1920s the ultimate service appeared to be within the grasp of Cunard. The possibility existed because of advances in marine technology of building two giant superliners that would be large enough and fast enough to maintain the weekly sailings by themselves: two great superliners sailing from Europe and America each week, passing each other in a majestic and thrilling mid-Atlantic meeting and racing on to their destination at nearly 30 knots. The vision was heroic; the realization in the face of the Great Depression would be extremely difficult.

The keel of an 80,000-ton Cunard liner was laid at John Brown's Shipyard on the Clyde on December 12, 1930, and given the yard number 534. Work proceeded on the enormous hull until December 10, 1931, when construction was suspended as a direct result of the economic devastation of the depression. Cunard could not build the ship without passenger and freight revenue, and trade on the North Atlantic had virtually dried up. The colossal hull of No. 534 rusting away on the Scottish slip was a gaunt reminder of how bad economic conditions were. Under the pressure of the depression, steamship lines collapsed in many trades. White Star had become British owned again after World War I but was undercapitalized and began to go bankrupt as the depression deepened. When Cunard approached the British government for aid in completing No. 534 and an appropriate sister ship, the terms offered involved a merger of the two foremost British-flag North Atlantic shipping lines. In February 1934 the Cunard-White Star Line was formed, and work resumed on No. 534 in April with the proposed launching date scheduled for September 26, 1934. Considerable excitement above and beyond the usual surrounded the launching. The merger of Cunard and White Star created a potential problem in naming the new ship because all Cunard vessels had ended in *ia* and all White Star ships ended in *ic*. Few guessed the solution that had been devised until Her Majesty Queen Mary ascended to the launching platform and at the appointed time in the ceremony christened the giant hull *Queen Mary*. A gracious monarch had consented to give the new superliner her own name in recognition of the fact that the ship had become a symbol of national unity and determination in the face of the dark clouds of the depression.

The merger of Cunard and White Star required drastic rationalization of the combined fleet. In the depths of the depression it was difficult enough to maintain a single first-class fleet, let alone twice the tonnage. The *Mauretania* was withdrawn in the fall of 1934, the *Olympic* in the spring of 1935, and the *Majestic* and *Homeric* early in 1936, while the *Berengaria, Aquitania,* and *Queen Mary* maintained the service from 1936 to 1938.

The *Queen Mary's* maiden voyage to New York, under the command of Captain Sir Edgar T. Britten, began in Southampton on May 27, 1936. There was an intermediate stop at Cherbourg. Wherever she went, the new liner was greeted by crowds and unprecedented enthusiasm. Her entry into New York Harbor was a publicity triumph, with the superliner accepting the thunderous salutes of all the vessels in the harbor and a flotilla of escorts seeing her to her North River pier. The *Queen Mary* overwhelmingly was the largest British-flag ship at 80,774 tons and with a length of 1,019 feet, five inches and a breadth of 118 feet, six inches. These statistics also compared favorably with her greatest competitor, the giant *Normandie* of the French Line, which emerged from the builder's yard at 79,280 tons, with a length of 1,029 feet, four inches by 117 feet, nine inches. Her tonnage was subsequently increased by various modifications to 83,423. The *Normandie* had commenced her maiden sailing from Le Havre on May 29, 1935, nearly a year ahead of the *Queen Mary*. She took the Blue Riband of the North Atlantic in 1935 with crossings of four days, three hours, two minutes westbound at an average speed of 29.98 knots and four days, three hours, twenty-five minutes eastbound at an average speed of 30.31 knots. The French liner thus became the first vessel to push the speed over thirty knots for an entire Atlantic crossing, and the *Queen Mary* faced a real challenge.

Cunard found it necessary to state that their new liner would not compete for the Blue Riband but simply would seek to perform up to the highest standards consistent with a regular service. On the crossings of August 20–24, 1936 (westbound), and August 26–30 (eastbound), the *Queen Mary* steamed across from Bishop's Rock to Ambrose in four days, twenty-seven minutes at 30.14 knots and returned in three days, twenty-three hours, fifty-seven minutes at 30.63 knots, becoming the first ship ever to complete back-to-back 30-knot crossings and the first vessel to lower the time below four days for a crossing. Thereafter the *Queen Mary* and *Normandie* exchanged the Blue Riband between them before the Cunarder proved herself slightly the faster in 1938 by a fraction of a knot.

Cunard had received sufficient funds to underwrite the building of the sister ship to the *Queen Mary* and the keel of this vessel was laid on December 4, 1936, at John Brown's. The launching of the new liner occurred after the accession of King George VI and Queen Elizabeth (the Queen Mother), and the new queen was asked by Cunard to launch the second liner. Accordingly, on September 27, 1938, Queen Elizabeth came to Clydebank and gave her name to the new ship.

In September 1939 a world war interrupted regular Cunard services for the second time in the century. The *Queen Mary* immediately was taken over as a fast troopship. The *Queen Elizabeth* was still being fitted out on the Clyde. She was too valuable a target to remain in that vulnerable position, and at the earliest possible opportunity, March 2, 1940, she sailed for "trials," which resulted in her safe arrival in New York five days later. The *Queens* between

The *Queen Elizabeth* (1940–1968) never made a traditional maiden voyage. Because the ship was considered to be vulnerable to air attack during World War II, it was secretly decided that she would sail to the United States as soon as possible after building was completed. When she departed the Clyde, her captain and crew had no idea their destination was New York until they were well clear of the coast. She was sold to American interests in 1968 and then to the C. Y. Tung Group in 1970. Renamed *Seawise University*, she caught fire in Hong Kong harbor in 1972 and became a total loss.

them ferried 320,000 of the 865,000 United States troops landed in Britain before the invasion of Europe. General Dwight D. Eisenhower credited the two giant Cunarders with shortening the war in Europe by a full year through their unique ability to transport 15,000 troops at a time. The loan of the two largest ships in the world by Britain to the United States constituted a significant reverse "lend-lease" factor during World War II and a major contribution on the part of Britain to the American war effort. Together the *Queens* carried the astonishing number of 1,622,054 passengers during the war years and steamed 1,150,406 miles.

Although all of the Cunard fleet was involved in the war, two ships rendered major service: the *Mauretania*, 35,738 tons, which had entered service in 1939 and been given the name of her famous predecessor, and the aging *Aquitania*, which would have been retired when the *Queen Elizabeth* entered service had the war not intervened. The old *Aquitania* became the only major ship of the Cunard fleet to serve in World Wars I and II, continuing her service until 1950.

As soon as possible after the war, Cunard refurbished the *Queens*, and in 1946 the two-ship transatlantic service became a reality. Sir Percy Bates, chairman of the Cunard-White Star, whose vision had seen the creation of the two *Queens*, collapsed and died at Southampton shortly after the maiden sailing of the *Queen Elizabeth* from her home port, on October 16, 1946. When entering the regular North Atlantic service of the Cunard Line in 1946 the *Queen Elizabeth*, at 83,673 tons and 1,031 feet long, held the distinction of being the largest passenger liner ever built. The *Queen Mary* and the *Queen Elizabeth* maintained Cunard's first-class service for the next twenty-one years and established an enviable record of popularity. The total number of passengers carried by the *Queen Elizabeth* during her first full year in service was 102,292 during the course of twenty-three round-trips—an average of 2,224 per trip. The healthy financial picture of the Cunard Line in 1947 permitted them to buy out the remaining White Star interest. The shares were passed over on January 21, 1948, and the company name changed back to the Cunard Steam-Ship Company Limited. The *Britannic* (1930), last of the White Star ships, retained the buff funnels with the black crown of White Star until she was retired in 1960, but little else remained of what once had been one of the world's foremost steamship lines.

The *Mauretania* was reconditioned as well and rejoined the fleet in April 1947, while new tonnage included the 13,345 ton *Media*, the first new postwar passenger vessel; a sister ship, the *Pathia*; and the spectacular 34,183-ton *Caronia*, in 1949. Other prewar ships that slowly returned to commercial activity were the *Ascania* (14,013 tons), *Britannic* (modified tonnage 27,650), *Samaria* (19,602 tons), *Sythia* (19,730 tons), and *Franconia* (20,158 tons). The dock at Cherbourg was repaired after war damage by May 1952, and continental passengers could now be embarked directly on to the biggest Cunarders without the use of tenders to ferry them out to the ships. A new train, the Cunarder, was created to run between Waterloo Station, London, and the Southampton docks in order to expedite the movement of thousands of passengers to the ships. It began service for the July 2, 1952, sailing. The departure of the Cunarder from cavernous Waterloo Station always was a most dramatic moment as the distinguished bass voice of the train announcer indicated that the boat train for R.M.S. *Queen Mary*, sailing from Southampton to New York, was about to leave. The excitement was incalculably enhanced if other liners also were sailing and a long series of boat trains for other ships also were being called. The train ride through the rolling English countryside to the Southampton docks provided a brief interlude and a means of catching one's breath for the thrill of embarkation on a ship that had come to be so much more than a living bit of history and tradition.

In the early 1950s Cunard also ordered a quartet of 22,000-ton liners, *Saxonia* (1954), *Ivernia* (1955), *Carinthia* (1956), and *Sylvania* (1957), all of which were intended for use in service between Britain, Quebec, and Montreal, although they took some New York sailings during the winter months. The interior fittings of the four ships were luxurious for the 110 to 154 first-class passengers but out of step for the times in connection with the 800 tourist

The *Caronia* (34,183 tons, 715 feet by 91 feet, 22 knots) was Cunard's "Green Goddess," built especially as a luxurious long cruise liner and only occasionally serving on the North Atlantic. The *Caronia* took Cunard's World Cruise, or long cruise, every year, from her commissioning in 1949 through 1967, and was the largest unit of postwar fleet prior to the *QE2*.

class cabins, most of which lacked private facilities. Cunard realized this, and during 1963 the *Saxonia* and *Ivernia* were refurbished as cruising liners with greatly refined accommodations. They were renamed *Carmania* and *Franconia* and painted in the light green cruising colors made popular by the *Caronia*. The *Carinthia* and the *Sylvania* were laid up in 1967 and then sold to the Sitmar Line in 1968 and renamed the *Fairsea* and the *Fairwind*. The *Carmania* and the *Franconia* proved to be popular Bermuda and Caribbean cruise liners, but a combination of labor problems and the rising cost of fuel forced their retirement in 1971. Ultimately they were sold to the Soviet Union in 1973 and renamed the *Leonid Sobinov* and the *Fedor Shalyapin*. The earning capacity of the Canadian quartet was severely affected by the advent of jet aircraft after 1958, as were the revenues from the *Queens*.

The year 1958 was the last time that more passengers crossed the North Atlantic by sea than by air. The Industrial Revolution as applied to transportation made another great leap forward as three-and-a-half-day Blue Riband passages, even by the superliner *United States*, which in 1952 took the record from the *Queen Mary*, became inconsequential in the face of air flights reckoned in hours. At the same time the policies of the British government toward taxation of business profits and the reserves necessary to finance new construction continuously wore down the resources of an old, established firm like Cunard. The Cunard Steamship Company began to lose money on its passenger operations at an ever-increasing rate. Drastic actions had to be taken in many areas, but the most critical problem facing the line in the early 1960s was what action to take with the first-class North Atlantic service. The *Queen Mary* and the *Queen Elizabeth* remained remarkable vessels, but they were aging and their fuel consumption at nearly 1,000 tons a day represented an enormous expense.

A set of plans for a new liner had been drawn up in the late 1950s and the ship had been dubbed *Q3*. If built that liner would have been around 75,000 tons and basically a modernized version of the *Queens*. The times had changed radically, however, and the *Q3* design was scrapped in favor of a slightly smaller and more versatile vessel capable of alternating at will between the North Atlantic and cruising—*Q4*. John Brown and Company won the contract, which was signed on December 30, 1964, and the keel was laid down on July 5, 1965—almost exactly 125 years after the maiden voyage of the *Britannia*. Plans were made to rationalize the fleet to recognize the facts of the maritime world. In line with this the *Mauretania* was scrapped in the fall of 1965. Matters worsened before the new construction could be completed, and Sir Basil Smallpeice, who had a wealth of business experience, was brought in as chairman of Cunard in November 1965. In order to raise additional funds the Cunard headquarters were transferred from Liverpool to London and the Cunard buildings in Liverpool, London, and New York were sold, while Cunard ticket offices were replaced by agencies in many cities. The 1965 figures revealed that Cunard had lost £2,700,000 on passenger ship operations and made only £900,000 on freight operations, for a net loss of £1,800,000. No company could stand that loss, finance a new ship, and still survive. Accordingly, the difficult decision was made to withdraw the *Queen Mary* at the end of the 1967 summer season and the *Queen Elizabeth* late in 1968 just prior to delivery of the new ship.

The *Queen Mary* brought the astonishing sum of £1,230,000 when sold to the city of Long Beach, California. She sailed from Southampton under the command of Commodore G. T. Marr for the last time on September 16, 1967, with 1,040 passengers on board for a cruise to California around Cape Horn since she was too large to transit the Panama Canal. The Cunard "Green Goddess" *Caronia* was retired in November 1967 and led a checkered life until sold for scrapping in 1974, only to be wrecked and sunk at Guam during a storm while under tow to a Chinese yard. The *Queen Elizabeth* maintained the North Atlantic service by herself during 1968, alternating sailings with the *France* of the French Line in a gentlemen's agreement not to have both big ships on the same side of the Atlantic. She was withdrawn from service on November 4, 1968, and sold to a group who intended to use her as a floating attraction in Port Everglades, Florida. This plan ultimately collapsed, as did a subsequent venture, and finally the ship was offered for auction. It looked as though she would be scrapped when C. Y. Tung, the Hong Kong shipping magnate,

The *Queen Mary* inspired many artists, but this painting by John Nicholson of Leeds is one of the best. She is shown on the North Atlantic, steaming along at 29 knots on a normal crossing. She would maintain the weekly service in peacetime from 1936 to 1967, when she was retired and sold to the city of Long Beach, California, for use as a maritime museum and hotel.

bought her. Tung intended to renovate and refurbish her as a floating university and rename her *Seawise University*. The reconstruction was nearly completed at Hong Kong when a mysterious fire broke out on January 9, 1972, and the giant liner turned on her side and burned for days in Hong Kong Harbor, becoming a total loss. She since has been scrapped — an unfortunate end for the largest passenger liner ever built.

The drastic fleet rationalization on the part of Cunard was the only option open to the line if it was going to survive. Time, money, and changing tastes were telling arguments against the older ships, as well as the enormous rise in fuel costs, which would be even more critical in the decade to come. By late 1968 the fortunes, future, and survival of the Cunard Steam-Ship Company lay with the spectacular new *Queen Elizabeth 2*.

CHAPTER TWO

The Ordering and Building of the *QE2*

The decision to invest £25 million in a project would certainly not be an easy one to make. When an industry is under acute stress as the result of changes beyond its control and a revolutionary new approach to design and technology is required, the strain of such a move would be tremendous. This was the situation when the management of the Cunard Line faced the issue of what type of vessel should replace the *Queen Mary* and the *Queen Elizabeth* in the late 1950s and early 1960s.

Official public notice of plans to replace the *Queens* occurred with the announcement in the House of Commons on April 8, 1959, by Harold Watkinson, ministry of transport, that negotiations were under way with Cunard to try to maintain first-class North Atlantic service. The previous month, Colonel Denis H. Bates told the annual meeting of Cunard that the future of the North Atlantic service had been placed before the government. Particular notice was taken of the fact that the United States government built the liner *United States* at a cost in excess of $75,000,000 and then made the vessel available to the U.S. Lines, Cunard's competition, for less than $34,000,000. "Faced with the overwhelming odds of ever-increasing governmental subsidies to our competitors on the score of national prestige," Bates commented, "your board have decided it is impossible to continue under such unequal and unfair competition to free enterprise." The *Queens* were described as "full of life," but they could not be run forever, and the *Queen Mary* probably would be well over thirty before her replacement would put to sea. Competitively that was not advantageous to the Cunard Line.

The government group given the responsibility for evaluating the situation was the Chandos committee, which began with the assumption that two liners ultimately would be built to replace the *Queens* and maintain the existing service. The recommendation of the Chandos committee on June 1, 1960, was in favor of construction of a 75,000-ton liner with a length of 990 feet and a service speed of 29 $\frac{1}{2}$ knots capable of carrying 2,270 passengers. The estimated cost in 1959 was £25 million to £30 million, with up to £18 million being provided by a low-interest government loan. On October 10, 1960, some five months later, Ernest Marples, then minister of transport, announced the government's acceptance of the recommendations of the Chandos committee. Vociferous opposition occurred almost immediately from some members of parliament who regarded the loan as an unprecedented subsidy, and from a vocal group of Cunard stockholders who regarded the building of another giant Atlantic liner in the face of competition from the jet airplane as insane. Certainly the *Q3*, as the new liner was dubbed, would enjoy only limited cruising flexibility during the winter months. The winter payloads on the older *Queens* had already fallen to virtually nothing, and every time such a ship left port she was destined to cast off into a sea of red ink. On one occasion the giant *Queen Elizabeth* made a winter crossing with only sixty-three passengers.

The whole complexion of the North Atlantic was undergoing radical change. In 1957 the division of passengers between ships and airlines was roughly 50 percent to 50 percent. By 1965 the ratio had changed to 14 percent to 86 percent and the number of individuals crossing by sea had dropped from over one million to around 650,000. In the same period the airlines saw their figures soar to over four million as the jets reduced the Atlantic crossing to a matter of hours. Even the British government investment concessions after 1957 meant little because the Cunard Line had to make substantial profits in order to take advantage of the new arrangement. The days of high profits were gone with the existing fleet.

Cunard endeavored to place itself in a more favorable position by acquiring British Eagle Airways in 1959, but that concern ran afoul of the government policy to restrict competition with BOAC in 1961. Subsequently Cunard and BOAC reached a trading agreement that created BOAC-CUNARD to operate the principal British-flag air service on the North Atlantic. Cunard owned 30 percent of the new company and enjoyed increased profits between 1962 and 1965. By 1965 it was realized that a substantial new investment was going to be necessary to maintain a competitive edge in air travel. However, Cunard did not have the financial resources to build a new liner and order new airplanes at the same time. An agreement was reached in 1966 for BOAC to purchase Cunard's share of their joint operations for a price of £11$\frac{1}{2}$ million, thus putting Cunard in a better position to focus on shipping. Unfortunately, between 1960 and 1965 the passenger ships of the line lost £14.1 million, which was only partially offset by tax refunds. A total rethinking of the future of the maritime industry and Cunard's role in it was imperative. The debate over the nature of the new vessel had to be considered against this background of a financial crisis.

The introduction of the magnificent *France* of the French Line in 1962 and the pairing of that vessel with the *United States* of the U.S. Lines provided additional competition for the *Queens*. Cunard countered by canceling the *Queens'* annual summer refitting, which prior to this had cost them a round-trip at the height of the season. Cunard also took a hard look at their competition, particularly the highly successful *Rotterdam* (1959) of Holland-America Line, which had been designed both as a North Atlantic liner and as a cruise ship.

Sir John Brocklebank, chairman of Cunard, reluctantly announced on October 19, 1961, that the Cunard Line could not see its way clear to order the *Q3*. The plans for the 75,000-ton vessel were shelved forever because trading conditions could not justify the replacing of the *Queens* by similar tonnage. It was back to the drawing board. For over a year things looked grim, until it was announced in December 1962 that Cunard was deeply involved in plans for a smaller and more versatile liner. The new ship would be about 55,000 tons and capable of transiting most of the major waterways of the world, such as the Panama and Suez canals. It was to have a width of less than 110 feet and a length of less than 990 feet, the maximum allowed in order to pass through the Panama locks. By early summer 1963 plans for a ship were submitted to Marples at the ministry of transport once again. This time the government refused Cunard a special loan for the vessel but did not close the door to aid. Instead, it was suggested that Cunard reapply for assistance from a new loan fund, under the direction of Lord Piercy, that had been established to aid shipowners willing to place contracts with British yards. Cunard promptly did so and received assurances of a loan of £17,600,000 toward the cost of the new liner.

Plans were sent to the British yards interested in tendering for the ship on September 9, 1964. The earlier contract for the *Q3* almost assuredly would have gone to a consortium led by Vickers-Swan Hunter of Tyneside, but this was not to be the case now. Strict attention to cost and delivery times was imperative for Cunard when the bids were received on November 30, 1964. The winner was announced within one month and the contract for the new liner was signed on December 30, 1964, with John Brown (Clydebank) Ltd., which had quoted both the lowest price and the earliest delivery date: May 1968. The ship was described in glowing terms as capable of holding her own on the North Atlantic and also as being one of the most fabulous resorts in the world. She would be able to cruise anywhere and provide her passengers with a level of luxury unsurpassed by any competition.

The new ship was to cost £25,427,000, with an escalation clause to cover inflationary factors. Although £17,600,000 was going to be loaned by the government, Cunard had to find the money to pay the builders in order to receive

The keel laying for Yard No. 736 was scheduled for July 2, 1965, but the 180-ton block of steel involving three keel sections welded together would not budge on that day, and the cranes began to move instead. Nevertheless, the keel-laying ceremony went ahead as scheduled at John Brown's. (Photo courtesy of the John Maxtone-Graham Collection.)

substantial advance payments of £4,000,000. To do this, the company found no alternative but to mortgage the fleet. Accordingly, five liners and six cargo ships were mortgaged to a consortium of British banks to raise the money. It was a difficult and vulnerable time for the line, further complicated by the serious illness and subsequent retirement in November 1965 of Sir John Brocklebank as chairman. His successor was Sir Basil Smallpeice, the energetic and respected former general manager of BOAC.

The goal for the new ship was to create a vessel capable of presenting and selling to the public a whole new way of life. There was no question anymore of her being just a means of getting from point A to point B. Conditions in the travel industry had changed so drastically that to be successful the new liner had to be viewed as a floating luxury resort, a five-star hotel with the additional advantage of being able to go anywhere in the world. Happily for Cunard, the tremendous innovations in design, materials, and construction techniques in the 1950s and 1960s made possible the creation of a ship that could capture the attention of the space-age traveling public.

July 2, 1965, was established as the day on which the first section of the keel would be laid at John Brown's for the vessel given the yard number 736. The berth to be used was the same from which the two earlier *Queen* liners had been launched. The first welded steel section of the keel was in one gigantic piece weighing 180 tons, 117 feet long, 23 feet wide, and 6 feet 3 inches high. When the first attempt was made to slide the 180-ton unit onto the greased oak blocks of the slipway, it had a mind of its own. The keel section refused to budge—instead, the crane mounting blocks began to move as it took up the strain. Over the next few days, the lifting and anchoring arrangements on the crane were reinforced and the first section of the keel was moved into position on July 5, 1965, while the 125th anniversary celebration of the Cunard Line was still under way. Special menus graced the tables of diners the previous

The 125th anniversary of the Cunard Line was commemorated with a special menu that surveyed the history and status of the fleet on July 4, 1965. Preparations were simultaneously being made for the laying of the keel plate of a giant new superliner at John Brown's on the Clyde.

evening on the vessels of the fleet as the Cunard Line extolled the past and heralded the future with the keel laying of No. 736.

Already publicists were eager for details of the giant new Cunarder. Certainly her machinery was going to be revolutionary, as she was to be the largest twin screw ship in the world. Her three boilers were to produce superheated steam at 950 degrees Fahrenheit for turbines that would generate 110,000-shaft horsepower. All this was to be done with half of the fuel consumption of the old *Queens*. The electrical generators in the new liner were to create enough power to serve the needs of a city of over 20,000.

Extensive design work on the hull was carried out by the Cunard architects and the National Physical Laboratory. Then the staff at John Brown's also put the hull form of the ship through test after test in the yard's experimental tank and fed the results into a new IBM computer. The computer analyzed the statistics and fed back evaluations within an hour—a process that used to take weeks. Time was of the essence, and a tight organization was crucial to the financial success of the project, from the standpoint of the builders and the steamship line. John Rannie, managing director of John Brown, was a key individual at the shipyard, but George Parker, director, was the individual who kept a tight watch on the actual building and insured that materials were in place as required. Organization was greatly assisted by the ability of computers to keep track of the whereabouts and status of such things as the 100,000 different pieces of pipe the ship would need.

Cunard wanted to have their personal representative on the scene at John Brown's at the earliest possible opportunity. Accordingly, on December 7, 1966, at a management conference held in Winchester, it was announced that Captain William Eldon Warwick, relief captain of the *Queen Mary* and *Queen Elizabeth*, was being appointed master-designate of the new ship, effective immediately. At fifty-four, Warwick, a native of Birkenhead, was the youngest captain ever to be appointed master of a *Queen* liner. He had been with the line for thirty years, joining Cunard as third officer of the *Lancastria* in 1937.

Among the revolutionary aspects of the new ship was the use of 1,100 tons of welded aluminum in the superstructure. So much of the light metal had never been used before in marine construction, but the advantages in stability and reduction of weight were enormous. This was also the first time that aluminum was to be used as an integral part of the stress-bearing hull of a ship. Looking at the construction of the new ship from a fabricating point of view, one can consider an all-welded superstructure, like an all-welded hull, as a single piece made up of a large number of smaller sections. The sections were prewelded in the shipyard's shops and then moved to the building berth for assembly in the ship. The lightness of aluminum allowed great freedom in the size of prefabrication; the only limitation was due to the size of the doors

Captain William Eldon Warwick stands in front of his new command in December 1966, after seeing her for the first time at John Brown's on the Clyde. The launching date is nearly ten months away, but the 17,500 tons of steel plate in the hull already make it appear massive.

By September 29, 1966, fifteen months after the keel laying, 1,400 men were at work on the ship. The large stern frame weighing 62 tons was ready for positioning, and special sheer legs had to be positioned to lift the large casting that had been brought to the site by barge. The stern frame provides a secure housing for the rudder. (Photo courtesy of the John Maxtone-Graham Collection.)

Large sections of the new ship were prefabricated in different parts of the builder's yard. Here, the large steel bulbous bow is being lowered into position prior to being welded onto the existing hull structure.

through which they would have to pass to reach the building berth. The doors were 36 by 22 feet and could accommodate aluminum assemblies up to 12 tons. The result was that approximately 130 separate multi-ton pieces were welded together to create the superstructure of the new liner. Great care was taken with the attachment of the aluminum superstructure to the steel hull wherever the two metals came into contact in order to avoid corrosion

Although the hull is already towering above the town, there are still more decks, the bridge, mast, and funnel to add. This photograph shows the steel superstructure up to the Quarter Deck, above which construction continued in the lighter metal aluminum.

through electrolytic action. The firm of John S. Craig & Co. Ltd., Glasgow, developed a flexible epoxy liquid that was applied to one of the two surfaces after an elaborate cleaning and curing process. The two metals were then riveted together and in the heating process a tight seal was formed prohibiting contact between the two metals and the intrusion of water into the joint.

The top four of the thirteen decks in the ship are aluminum. The first prefabricated aluminum unit of the Upper Deck was lowered into position on the steel Quarter Deck on January 21, 1967. Within eighteen weeks the Upper Deck was well advanced and within six months the superstructure was clearly emerging. When the aluminum superstructure was completed the savings in weight to the new ship gave her a seven-foot reduction in draft over the older *Queens*, an incalculable asset in view of Cunard's desire to use the vessel extensively for cruising.

A unique aspect of the liner was the installation of a computer with a data logging system. When the decision was made to see how much of the work of the liner could be handled by a computer system, negotiations began with the British Ship Research Association, resulting in the equipping of the ship with a Ferranti Argus 400 computer.

By April 1967, the huge hull of No. 736 soared 95 feet into the Clyde skyline. The assembly schedule called for the installation of 30 to 35 tons of steel and aluminum a week into the ship. (Photo courtesy of the John Maxtone-Graham Collection.)

A major setback in the proceedings occurred in July 1967 when John Brown informed Sir Basil Smallpeice that the cost of the new ship would probably be in the range of £28 ½ million, up some £3 million from the original contract price. Simultaneously, Philip Bates, Cunard's managing director, came up with the news that there would be another £3 ½ million loss on the passenger ships in 1967. Sir Basil Smallpeice had no choice but to inform the Board of Trade, overseeing the building aid program, that the sum guaranteed to the line by the government was no longer adequate and that construction of the ship would have to cease unless additional funds were made available. Complicating the issue was the fact that the announced launching day was September 20, 1967. Her Majesty Queen Elizabeth II had consented to launch the liner in the proud tradition of her grandmother, Queen Mary, and her mother, Queen Elizabeth, the Queen Mother. The Cunard board of directors met under tense conditions on September 14 as they awaited word on whether or not the government would agree to increasing the loan. The situation was so critical that a negative response might force the board to cease operations and sell off the assets for whatever they might bring rather than lose more money. To the relief of everyone concerned, Harold Lever, financial secretary to the treasury, sent Sir Basil a note while the board was in session indicating that the government would increase the loan to Cunard from £17,600,000 to £24,000,000, permitting the launch to go forward as planned.

The rumors about the name for No. 736 were as numerous as they had been for the launching of the *Queen Mary* thirty years before. The old story was trotted out about Sir Percy Bates, then chairman of Cunard, and King George V

The hull has now been given the final coat of paint and is almost ready for launching. The bridge, mast, and funnel will be added after she has been moved to the fitting-out berth.

The rudder of No. 736 weighs 70 tons, is 27 feet, 6 inches long and 23 feet, 6 inches deep. The surface area equals 482 square feet, and the hinge pin alone is 7 feet high, 26 inches in diameter, and weighs 5 tons. The rudder is filled with plastic foam to make it leakproof and to prevent internal corrosion. (Photo courtesy of the John Maxtone-Graham Collection.)

discussing the name for the first *Queen* liner. Supposedly Sir Percy was thinking of the name *Queen Victoria* (with an *ia* name ending) when he asked the king for permission to name the new Cunarder after "our most illustrious Queen." The monarch responded that he would be delighted to ask Queen Mary when they returned to the palace. That story almost assuredly is untrue

Near to the launching day in September 1967, the two massive six-bladed propellers are installed. The rudder also is in place for the launch. The force of the propellers against the water as she goes down the ways will assist in slowing her momentum as she makes her bow to the world. Note the tiny figure of a workman beneath the 70-ton rudder; other people are clustered near the port propeller. (Photo courtesy of the Frank O. Braynard Collection.)

and many good authorities have tried to put it to rest. There would not be the possibility of such a problem this time. There was no question what Sir Basil and the Cunard board desired. The name was discussed with Lord Adeane, the queen's private secretary, and it was decided simply to ask that the new ship be named *Queen Elizabeth*, because by the time of her commissioning both of the earlier *Queens* would be withdrawn from service and she could assume the name vacated by one of her predecessors.

Launching day on the Clyde was pleasant, as the crowds milled around the launching site or lined the riverbank opposite to watch the show. Her Majesty Queen Elizabeth II moved to the front of the launching platform and was handed an envelope by John Rannie with the name of the ship inside. This was a tradition because many years before someone purportedly had forgotten the name of the ship about to be launched. The envelope remained unopened as the queen stepped forward and uttered the words:

> "I name this ship *Queen Elizabeth the Second*. May God Bless her and all who sail in her."

Sir Basil Smallpeice was overjoyed at the sovereign's alteration of the name.* He could not have been more delighted with having the third of the great royal Cunarders named in this manner. The decision promptly was made to style the giant liner *Queen Elizabeth 2* using the numeral two to differentiate the ship from the sovereign.

*Sir Basil Smallpeice, *Of Comets and Queens* (Shrewsbury, 1980).

The two giant six-bladed propellers, weighing 31.75 tons each and 19 feet in diameter, have been delivered to the yard by the manufacturers. They will be connected to the tail shaft before the ship is launched.

Her Majesty Queen Elizabeth II has just named No. *736* the *Queen Elizabeth 2*, on September 20, 1967, and the giant Cunarder rushes toward her element without a hitch in the proceedings.

The goal of Cunard and John Brown had been to get the *Queen Elizabeth 2* in service in time to make the most of the 1968 summer season on the North Atlantic, but that was not to be. By the launching date it was obvious that it would be impossible to complete the complex task of fitting out the huge liner in time for the late spring 1968 sailings. The schedule was pushed back to the

In addition to the shipyard workers, thousands of spectators lined the banks of the Clyde to witness what would become the last launching of a transatlantic liner in British maritime history.

autumn of 1968 and this provided the opportunity for a major transformation of the ship.

A debate had been raging between those in favor of three classes and those who felt that since the future of the ship lay in cruising as well as the North Atlantic, she should be a two-class ship. The principal advantage of two classes over three was that the public rooms of the ship could be much larger. The feeling in America had been that in a ship carrying first, cabin, and tourist it was still possible to sell the cabin class accommodation in sufficient numbers to warrant carving up the liner three ways. However, in Britain and among the Cunard staff employed at sea the two-class vessel seemed most practicable and profitable.

Captain William Law of the *Carmania* wrote on February 6, 1964:

> Cabin class has no place in the future. The argument is often put forward that the cabin class in the *Queens* is well booked; this is merely due to the fact that the tourist class is well below standard and that number of people who cannot afford the first class fare feel that they desire something better than the present tourist class. In a new ship with a well designed attractive tourist class there will be no need for the "middle of the road" passenger to look for anything beyond the tourist class.

The *QE2* is now afloat for the first time. As she entered the water, seven tugs were standing by to ensure that she cleared the bank on the opposite side of the river and then to tow her to the fitting-out berth.

Afloat in the fitting-out berth, the *QE2* draws about 25 feet in the water, which gives the cranes sufficient height to add the remaining superstructure. At the same time, the ship's name, having been revealed at the launching, is now being painted on the port bow.

An aerial view of the John Brown Shipyard along the Clyde River, Clydebank, Scotland. Yard No. 736 dominates the shipyard and soars far enough into the air that airplanes approaching Prestwich Airport, Glasgow, regard it as a landmark. The hull rests on the same building berth used for the *Queen Mary* and the *Queen Elizabeth*.

Another telling argument was that as a three-class ship the *Queen Elizabeth 2* would be able to accommodate up to 2,000 passengers, whereas if there were only going to be two classes, the number could be increased to 2,030 and the number of staff decreased. Another problem involving passenger capacity and classes was how to divide the ship, and various studies were made to try to resolve this. Finally, under the direction of Sir Basil Smallpeice the two-class proponents won the day on the basis of the emphasis to be placed on cruising.

The design team for the new liner was led by D. N. Wallace, chief naval architect for Cunard, whose life revolved around the new liner for nearly a decade before she was launched. Dan Wallace received a vast amount of information from all over the world as hotels and liners were evaluated for ideas to make the new ship efficient and luxurious. The main requests for the new ship from all sources were: more single and two-bedded rooms linked with adjoining rooms; elimination of upper bunks whenever possible; more outside cabins with natural daylight; private showers, baths, and toilets in every cabin; ample wardrobe and drawer space; good lighting in the cabins; efficient sound insulation and absence of vibration; a wide range of public rooms so that passengers might enjoy communal entertainment in the nightclubs and the theaters or solitude and quietness in the Card Room, library, or reading room; greatly enlarged exterior deck space and swimming pools for cruising; and carefully planned, colorful, and stimulating facilities for children.

James Gardner was appointed as exterior design coordinator after construction had started. It was his task to bring order and unity to the features of the hull and superstructure that had already been established by the naval architects. The basic challenge, as Gardner saw it, was to create a ship that was both attractive and practical and to avoid having it look like an apartment block. This was achieved by a delicate balance of converging lines fore and aft centered on the bridge as a focal point. The optical illusion of subtle curves and grace was achieved. Nuances of color and design were combined in the color scheme of the lifeboats and their background in order to minimize their visual disruption of the clean lines of the ship. Research had shown that the funnel should be tall and slender to avoid fumes and soot falling onto the deck. Accordingly, the traditional fat Cunard funnel was abandoned. At the time of building, the designers thought the color red was unsuitable so it was painted white for the first few years of the ship's life.

Dennis Lennon was responsible for coordinating the work of the ten-man team of top designers involved in styling the interiors of over 1,400 public rooms and cabins on the liner. Their design created a unified and integrated interior reflecting the best of contemporary thought and manufacture. Lennon had been brought in through the invitation of Lady Brocklebank when Sir John Brocklebank was chairman of Cunard. There had been some disgruntlement over such an important appointment's being granted without a design competition. Lennon's achievements soon stifled all dissent.

Significant of the change in philosophy in connection with the design and layout of the new ship was the desire to open as many of the public rooms as possible to a view of the sea. The attitude of the previous hundred years had been to make passengers crossing on a great transatlantic liner forget that they were at sea by the nature of their surroundings. Opulent public rooms gave the illusion of "life as usual" with the assumption that one might never have left port. When ships were the only means of crossing the ocean and the trip was often as much dreaded as appreciated, it was appropriate to camouflage the fact that the passenger was at sea. Millionaires could feel as comfortable in the great public rooms and suites of the *Aquitania* as in their own homes. It was possible, of course, to go out on deck, but it was desirable for only a few months of the year, and even then it was an invigorating and, for some, an unpleasant experience. In contrast, the design team for the *Queen Elizabeth 2* was actively encouraged to emphasize the sea. The passengers who traveled by transatlantic liners, Cunard reasoned, did so by choice rather than because of lack of alternatives. Hence the great restaurants of the liner were placed high in the ship so that passengers dining on gourmet cuisine could have the best of both worlds—a grand hotel and an ocean vacation. Furthermore, the basic nature of the new liner was that she was to be an "open ship" operating without class distinctions whenever she was cruising. Eliteness would be available through cabin selection and restaurant assignment for those who desired it. The overall expenditure for interior design work and outfitting was about £3,000,000 ($8,400,000), but, as Dennis Lennon said, "the public judge a ship by what has been done in the interior." The desire was to make the *QE2* second to none.

The interim report of the Cunard Line for the half-year ending June 30, 1968, was the most encouraging news that Sir Basil Smallpeice, or any Cu-

Late spring 1968 sees the bridge in place, still minus its wings, and the funnel has been seated, but there is no mast. The name *Queen Elizabeth 2* is emblazoned on the hull with the uniquely modern designation that would make the *QE2* famous.

One of the giant cranes is working through the turbine hatch aft of the funnel that descends directly to the engine room of the liner. Lifeboats are in place on the starboard side of the Boat Deck, and painting is under way. A dry-cargo bulk carrier can be seen under construction behind the *Queen*.

nard chairman for a decade, had been able to offer employees and stockholders. The slimming down of the passenger fleet by the removal from service and sale of the *Queen Mary*, *Caronia*, *Carinthia*, and *Sylvania* had resulted in a profit of £2,576,000 on a total passenger and freight revenue of £24,565,000. The figures for the previous year had shown a net loss of £2,031,000 for an actual turnaround of £3.1 million. The high prices brought by the Cunard tonnage that had been sold made it possible for the company to inform the British government that it did not need the remaining £4 million of the £24 million loan made available to them in September 1967.

The fitting out of the ship went on as rapidly as possible with an army of some 3,000 Scottish workers employed on board. By the time of the launch

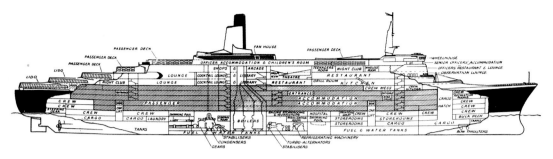

The "*Q4*" plans in a cutaway were available at the time of the launch on September 20, 1967, but, of course, no name could be attached to them; hence she could only be described as "the new 58,000-ton Cunarder." Later it would be realized that the *Queen Elizabeth 2* would weigh in at well over 65,000 tons, which would create some cause for concern until assurances were given that this would not curtail the range of her potential employment.

17,500 tons of steel from Colvilles of Glasgow, worth more than £1,000,000, had been used; so had £500,000 worth of aluminum from Alcan. Generators and other electrical equipment ordered from AEI were worth another £500,000, and air-conditioning equipment from Carrier capable of withstanding tropical sunshine was worth another £750,000. The bills grew apace with the ship.

A critical desire of Cunard was to have the *Queen Elizabeth 2* delivered on time so that the maximum advantage could be made of advance scheduling and publicity. As early as December 1966 it appeared obvious that the liner would not be completely finished in time for the spring-summer 1968 season. In determining the commissioning schedule, two most critical problems were how much loading of stores onto the ship could be done at the shipyard prior to delivery at Southampton and how long of a trial period would be required at sea after the ship's delivery (with guests on board but no fare-paying passengers) before the ship could begin commercial service. The hotel department, in particular, was concerned that all furnishings be placed on board before leaving the shipyard. Furthermore, a catering storing period spread over some three months was regarded as imperative before leaving the shipyard. The hotel department also felt that two eight-day cruises with company guests should be undertaken in order to get all systems fully tested and operational. Each section of the passenger accommodations was to be locked and secured as soon as it was finished.

The technical director, Thomas Kameen, led a team of seven Cunard engineers responsible for coordinating the design of the main turbines and auxiliary power plant, as well as all other main and minor machinery, including generators, evaporators, and the computer. Foremost among Kameen's concerns was the operation of the sprinkler system from the earliest possible moment, since more vessels have been lost from fires in yards and while fitting out than probably from any other single cause. The technical commissioning

A brilliant day on the Clyde shows the fitting-out basin at John Brown's, with the *QE2* nearing completion. Paint crews are at work on the port side, and the ship looks remarkably complete, although there still is no mast forward.

program was started nine months before the ship left John Brown's and included trials of all the major machinery as soon as possible. A proper sea trial had to include sufficient time to equal one North Atlantic round-trip voyage and take the ship into hot and humid weather so that the air-conditioning could be adjusted — a major problem on any new ship destined to operate both on the North Atlantic and in tropical waters. Cunard was under no delusions that the two-week shakedown cruise probably would produce a list of adjustments and defects requiring an additional two weeks in port before acceptance. The goal in December 1966 was to have the *QE2* ready for commercial service by January 1969.

In the period between December 1966 and May 1968 a financial collapse of the Clydebank shipyards occurred and a new organization known as Upper Clyde Shipbuilders, Ltd. was established to salvage whatever might prove economically viable. The projected £2,400,000 loss of John Brown and Company Ltd. on the *Queen Elizabeth 2* was the final blow to that old firm, although the writing had been on the wall for some time. This placed Cunard in the position of finishing a ship with a different firm. The instability of the times also produced substantial labor unrest, which did not make life any easier for Anthony Hepper, chairman of Upper Clyde Shipbuilders, as he tried to honor deadlines.

Sir Basil Smallpeice wrote to Hepper in May 1968 and emphasized the necessity of maintaining the November delivery deadlines:

> I know full well that you are very anxious that the ship should be delivered on time because the publicity attached to the ship world-wide is such that a late delivery of it could not rebound on Upper Clyde Shipbuilders. As far as we are concerned, the revenue potential of the ship, even in the winter, is of the order of £$^3/_4$ million a month, and even four weeks delay would therefore be a very serious matter from our point of view, to say nothing of your own.

Cunard was willing to accommodate Upper Clyde in almost any way if the *Queen* could just get to sea on time! Upper Clyde responded by making John Rannie, local director of UCS, solely responsible for the *QE2* with the power to do almost anything to get the ship ready for her trials. At the end of the summer Hepper set the tone for UCS by saying, "Although we are living in a very difficult situation at the moment, we are all very conscious of the extreme importance of this contract."

To the infinite relief of all concerned, just as dawn began to break over Scotland on November 19, 1968, the magnificent new *Queen Elizabeth 2* slowly eased her way out of the fitting-out berth at Clydebank and into the narrow river. Western Scotland had declared a holiday to watch the newest of the *Queens* majestically weave her way down the Clyde on a high tide. She needed all the water nature could supply, even if she did not draw as much as her predecessors. On the bridge was Captain William E. Warwick. Besides the normal complement of Cunard and Upper Clyde Shipbuilders personnel, he was joined by H.R.H. Prince Charles, the heir to the throne. As the *Queen Elizabeth 2* completed her turn and prepared to move downstream, Captain Warwick fulfilled the unspoken wish of his royal guest when he asked if he would like to blow the departure blast on the colossal whistles of the liner. Prince Charles was clearly delighted to do so. The *Queen*'s parting salute to her birthplace, where Her Majesty Queen Elizabeth II had launched her two years before, was given by the prince of Wales. Nothing could have been more appropriate.

Once in the Greenock Dry Dock, work on the completion of the *QE2* appeared to slow down. Five hundred carpenters were laid off one week and one hundred hired back the next, generating instability in the work force while the accommodations on the ship remained a shambles. Arrangements were made for the work force to remain on the ship so the fitting out could continue during the engine trials. The following week *QE2* left the dry dock and the engine trials commenced off the coast of Scotland. The turbines steadily built up

The *Queen Elizabeth 2* offers a magnificent panorama in this official Cunard Line photo of the liner taken while on trials in the English Channel. The open expanses of deck toward the stern have never been equaled in any other vessel.

speed until she was racing along at 29 $\frac{1}{2}$ knots, achieving this with two propellers, whereas the older *Queens* needed four, and with 50,000 less horsepower. The technical trials suddenly were interrupted by the discovery of an oil leak caused by a nonreturn valve that was permitting contaminated oil to leak into the high-pressure steam system. There was no choice but to return to dry dock and completely clean the entire main and auxiliary steam circulating systems, which required the better part of two weeks. This delayed the resumption of the technical trials until the week before Christmas, and a holiday charity cruise for the benefit of the National Society for Cancer Relief had to be canceled. As partial compensation to the society, Cunard made a contribution to its treasury. When the sea trials were resumed, the *Queen Elizabeth 2* delighted everyone by reaching 32.46 knots at full speed with no sign of trouble.

Hurried arrangements were then made to take the ship on her final acceptance trials on December 23 with 500 members of the Cunard organization and their families along as "guests" and guinea pigs. Few "guinea pigs" ever ended up working so hard, since much of the passenger accommodations still required cleaning. Two hundred Clyde workers went south with the ship in a desperate race to try to finish the most pressing carpentry work. Then, on the evening of December 24, as the liner steamed toward the Canary Islands, first the starboard high-pressure turbine and then the port turbine experienced problems. The initial thought was that the rotors were imbalanced, but the fault was far more serious than that. Sir Basil Smallpeice flew out to Los Palmas with Anthony Hepper of Upper Clyde Shipbuilders to inspect the situation. After hearing the extremely uncertain engineering report and seeing the unfinished state of the passenger accommodations, Sir Basil announced that Cunard would refuse to accept the liner until everything was corrected.

The *Queen Elizabeth 2* slowly steamed back to Southampton to something less than a triumphant arrival and accompanied by a flood of publicity. Nearly two hundred reporters had joined the ship in the Canary Islands for the trip back to England. However, the nature of the coverage was well balanced, as most writers stressed the magnificence of the vessel, even if she was experiencing teething troubles. The primary difficulty insofar as Cunard was concerned was to stimulate UCS to take immediate and drastic action to discover and solve the problem. By January 16, 1969, no positive identification of the turbine problem had been made, and John Brown Engineering, the manufacturers of the turbines, was estimating at least another three weeks' delay. In the face of that, Cunard canceled all future sailings. The company's position was simple:

> Cunard cannot accept delivery until after the ship's turbines
> have been thoroughly re-tested and proved in further basin
> trials, speed trials and a prolonged acceptance trial under
> maintained pressure, followed by further inspection. It is im-

At Southampton, on May 7, 1969, on her first visit to the ship since the naming ceremony, Her Majesty Queen Elizabeth II is escorted along the Boat Deck by the ship's first master, Captain William Warwick, accompanied by Sir Basil Smallpiece, Cunard's chairman.

possible to say when this programme of correction, testing and proving of the ship's power plant can be completed.

The problem with the turbines may have been a blessing in disguise. At least UCS could guarantee that the interior outfitting of the ship would be completed according to contract terms by the end of January. After consultation with a number of sources it was revealed that the problem with the turbines was that some of the blades continued to vibrate at an unacceptable pitch until they shattered and spread havoc everywhere in their path. Various strengthening efforts were made that solved this crucial problem. The result was a long, drawn-out process that was not near completion until mid-March. By March 16 it was announced by a greatly relieved Anthony Hepper that the *Queen Elizabeth 2* would undergo engine tests alongside her Southampton pier and then go to sea for speed trials in the English Channel.

The *QE2* went back into dry dock for cleaning and inspection and then out on a shakedown cruise at the end of March, during which all her machinery was tested and opened up for inspection. Everything being shipshape or, as Sir Basil put it, "Cunard-shape," the *Queen Elizabeth 2* finally was accepted by Cunard on April 20, 1969, at a final cost of £29,091,000.

The acceptance on April 20 permitted a mini-cruise to the Canary Islands to leave Southampton on April 22, which actually marks the beginning of *QE2*'s commercial service. Upon returning from the Canaries, the ship was provisioned for her maiden voyage. On the eve of her first transatlantic crossing Her Majesty Queen Elizabeth II and Prince Philip renewed their association with the ship by visiting her for a royal tour. The visit heralded what

The *QE2* in her earlier years, when the funnel was painted white, lies at anchor in a West Indies port where the passengers are ferried ashore by the ship's tenders.

Cunard was convinced would be the beginning of a brilliant career for Britain's largest liner. Captain William Warwick, master of the *QE2*, and Staff Captain George Smith received Her Majesty on board the ship. Among the ship's officers and heads of departments presented to the queen were Donald Wilson, chief engineer; Jack Marland, deputy chief engineer; and Mortimer Hehir, chief officer. The queen toured the bridge and the principal public rooms. The bust of Her Majesty, by the sculptor Oscar Nemon, was in the Queen's Room. The queen told of sitting for the sculptor on several occasions when he could not get the nature and position of the head to suit him; he had once unceremoniously wrenched it off. After the tour of the ship, a luncheon was served in the elite Princess Grill, with cold salmon as the main course, washed down with a 1962 Montrachet from the substantial cellars of the liner. The visit of Her Majesty to the *Queen Elizabeth 2* maintained a royal family tradition of three generations.

On May 2, 1969, nearly five years after her keel laying and two years after her launching, the *Queen Elizabeth 2* sailed from Southampton with 1,400 passengers for Le Havre and New York on her maiden voyage. What had appeared on occasions to be the impossible dream had become a glorious reality.

CHAPTER THREE

The Maiden Years

The maiden Atlantic crossing of the *Queen Elizabeth 2* was an appropriate introduction to the solid, comfortable luxury her passengers would enjoy in the future. The steaming time from Le Havre to the Ambrose light tower was four days, sixteen hours, thirty-five minutes, which gave an average speed of 28.02 knots. Early on the morning of May 7 the *QE2* was greeted by a flotilla of escorts as she neared the Verrazano Narrows Bridge. She was led into the harbor by the Coast Guard cutter *Morgenthau* while the U.S. Navy destroyer *Conway* took up position astern. Mayor John V. Lindsay of New York and a party of dignitaries boarded the *QE2* in the Lower Bay before noon, along with numerous members of the press. The feeling among those who came to greet her was that no vessel like her would ever be built again and that she represented the last of an era—the last great transatlantic liner. The gala parade up the harbor soon included hundreds of yachts and pleasure boats as well as a chartered ferry boat. In New York tradition, the fireboats were present with their fire pumps spraying water high into the air. The day had started cool and overcast but by noon the *Queen Elizabeth 2* was bathed in bright sunlight. She passed the Statue of Liberty and slowly steamed up the North River, exchanging thunderous salute after salute with other vessels in the harbor. As the afternoon started to wane, the *QE2* approached her berth at pier 92 and at 1512 hours "finished with engines" was rung. The maiden arrival of the *Queen Elizabeth 2* at New York had been one of the most spectacular welcoming celebrations that anyone could remember in the history of the port.

Many "arrival celebration" dinners were held all over New York City and on the *Queen*. One thousand guests of the Cunard Line at a supper dance en-

The *Queen Elizabeth 2* makes her majestic entrance to New York Harbor for the first time on May 7, 1969. Coast Guard cutters, fireboats, tugs, ferries, and yachts escort her as she exchanges salutes with other vessels. The crossing from Southampton to New York was accomplished in 4 days, 16 hours, and 35 minutes, at an average speed of 28.02 knots.

joyed the amenities of the new ship and exchanged stories about her illustrious predecessors. The *QE2* certainly was the biggest "happening" in New York, and those who came to see her were divided into two groups: those who had traveled on the old *Queens* and were astonished by the modern look of the new ship, and those who were social trendsetters and were impressed that a ship could look so exciting. Among the guests were members of the diplomatic corps to the United Nations, including the ambassadors from Britain, France, Sweden, the Soviet Union, Ghana, and Morocco, and a generous selection of prominent men and women from industry, transportation, and finance. Other guests included Mrs. John V. Lindsay, representing her husband, and the distinguished maritime author Walter Lord.

Many of the New York inaugural festivities on the *QE2* took place in the huge Double Down Room,* which, with its red, orange, chrome, and glass scheme, was strikingly different from anything in the old *Queens*. It was im-

*Now the Grand Lounge.

possible for the guests to realize that the Double Room was the tourist class public room when the ship operated with two classes on the North Atlantic. In assessing the new liner, one illustrious individual noted that it was characteristic of the times that there was virtually no noticeable difference between the first and tourist class public rooms. The subtle class distinctions were handled by a few discreet signs reserving areas for first class rather than the locked doors and barriers on previous vessels. The comments and reviews were mixed, but there was no question about the fact that the *Queen Elizabeth 2* broke new ground. If the *Queen Mary* in 1936 had been "evolutionary," there was no questioning the fact that the *Queen Elizabeth 2* in 1969 was "revolutionary." She therefore achieved exactly the effect that the directors of Cunard, and the ship's design team, had desired: She was unique. As John Quinn of the *Daily News* summed up his story, "the old queens are gone. Long live the Queen."

Upon arrival in Southampton on April 29, 1969, the *QE2* had the pleasure of a second visit from His Royal Highness, the Duke of Edinburgh. The purpose of the visit was to present the 1969 Council of Industrial Design awards. Among the 1969 winners were designers of the special dinning room chairs created for the *Queen Elizabeth 2*. While aboard, Prince Philip had a more thorough tour of the ship than he had had on his previous visit. He was shown some of the public rooms before being taken to the crew quarters, where he saw food being prepared for the crew mess. The tour also included the turbine control, engine, and boiler rooms. The popularity of the *QE2* among families traveling with young children grew steadily as it became known that the liner had some of the finest facilities and best organized entertainment programs ever created for children of all ages. Furthermore, if one was returning from a year or more in Europe with a family and did not want to restrict baggage, the *Queen* could end up as a bargain over the airline surcharges for overweight luggage. The *QE2* soon earned an enviable reputation as a spacious ship with comfortable accommodations and superb cuisine.

As far as her qualities as a good sea ship are concerned, the *Queen Elizabeth 2* may well represent the ultimate achievement in naval architecture. The beautiful, sheer lines of her hull below the waterline gave her a smooth entry into virtually any sea and resulted in the most stable performance of any of the great Atlantic liners. In addition, her stabilizers were designed and contoured precisely to compliment the hull lines of the ship and are able to operate under virtually any sea conditions and considerably reduce rolling, even in severe weather.

Her seaworthiness was put to the test in October 1969. The liner arrived in New York some ten hours late after having altered course several times during the North Atlantic crossing in order to avoid the worst of three major storm systems over the ocean. In meteorological terms, a complex depression with associated storm winds ranging up to Force 11 and accompanied by

On the maiden arrival of the *Queen Elizabeth 2* in New York, three Moran tugs were in attendance just to make sure that everything went perfectly as the brand new liner gracefully turned into her slip and came up against the old Cunard Line piers.

heavy west-southwesterly swells caused a speed reduction and delayed arrival. On October 18–19, relief Captain F. J. Storey took the *Queen* over 100 miles south, repeating this action on October 20–21 at reduced speed in order to minimize passenger discomfort. When yet a third storm in the same depression was encountered less than 600 miles from New York, there was not too much the ship could do to make up the time with the 110,000 horsepower at her command. The official Cunard report stated: "Considering the magnitude of the storms, it was considered that *QE2* made good headway and lived up to her reputation of being a good sea ship."

In October 1969 it was announced that Cunard had repaid £2 1/2 million of the government loan provided for the completion of the liner and that they would be in a position to repay £500,000 every six months of the outstanding balance of £12 million. Sir Basil Smallpeice commented:

> The fact that we have been able to make these repayments is clear evidence of Cunard's all-around progress and growing cash flow. I am glad that we are able to show in this practical way that the Government's confidence in Cunard's new direction and management was not misplaced.

Additional good news followed on November 3, 1969, when it was announced that the Cunard Line had decided to invite tenders for one, and possibly two, new 1,000-passenger ships. Although preference would be given to British yards, shipbuilders from all over the continent were invited to tender for the ships, with Cunard reserving the right to make a selection on the basis of price, delivery date, and credit terms.

The plans for the 1969–1970 winter season were for the *Queen Elizabeth 2* to have a series of seven ten-day Caribbean cruises from New York. Wherever

Outward bound from New York, the *QE2* passes the Statue of Liberty and heads toward the Verrazano Narrows Bridge. Passengers traveling on her for the first time are always convinced that the towering mast and funnel will not clear the under deck of the bridge. Several feet of clearance do exist even at high tide.

she went the *QE2* was given a royal welcome in a fabulous series of "maiden arrivals" that delighted passengers and islanders. At Kingston, Jamaica, the governor-general, Sir Clifford Campbell, and an official party were entertained on board while passengers were greeted by bands, mounted horsemen, and a festival atmosphere on shore. The series of Caribbean cruises proved popular, although even the 28-knot speed with which the *Queen* rushed her passengers south could not eliminate the penetrating cold of a New York sailing.

When the *Queen* returned from the Caribbean on February 5, 1970, she encountered two problems: the New York tugboats were on strike, and her pier was choked with ice. Captain W. E. Warwick had to ease his 963-foot ship steadily in and out of the slip four times in order to crunch the six-inch ice flows with her 65,000 tons and then, with the aid of the bow thrusters, berth her alongside the pier. Afterward the captain turned to his officers and said: "I never thought we would have to use a £30 million ship as an ice breaker."

Personal tragedy occasionally affects the lives of those who go to sea, and sometimes in a dramatic way. The first instance of a "man overboard" occurred on March 30, 1970, when the *Queen Elizabeth 2* was on passage from Barbados to Madeira. The ship was steaming along at 28 knots when at 1202 hours it was reported to the bridge that a man had been seen falling overboard. Immediately the speed was reduced and the rescue launch crew alerted. Within sixteen minutes *QE2* had completed a "Williamson turn," a maneuver that brought the ship onto her reciprocal course. During the turn, lookouts were scanning the area, and at 1249 hours an object was sighted floating in the water. Within five minutes the ship was stopped and the rescue launch was under way. At 1301 hours the body of a crew member was recov-

Few ports in the world are more highly regarded by cruise passengers than Charlotte Amalie, St. Thomas, Virgin Islands. As the Caribbean sun begins to set, the bow of the *Queen Elizabeth 2* points toward the exquisite setting of the resort hotel of Frenchman's Reef.

ered from the sea, but efforts to revive him proved unsuccessful. The launch was recovered by 1316 hours and the ship resumed her passage. Although the incident was unfortunate, it did serve to demonstrate the maneuverability of one of the largest ships in the world.

By coincidence, it had been arranged for stop trials to be carried out the following week in the presence of British Board of Trade surveyors for the purpose of verifying and checking the ability of the ship to stop under emergency conditions. These "emergency stop trials" were undertaken on April 5, 1970, while on passage from Lisbon to Le Havre. At 0918 hours the *Queen* was steaming through the ocean at $29\frac{1}{2}$ knots when the full-astern order was given. Within 4 minutes at 0922 hours, the forward momentum of the ship had been reduced to $8\frac{1}{2}$ knots and both engines were moving astern. By 0924 hours and $\frac{1}{2}$ minute, $6\frac{1}{2}$ minutes following "full astern," the *Queen* had stopped dead in the water, and within an additional 2 minutes, at 0926 hours and $\frac{1}{2}$, she was making $4\frac{1}{2}$ knots astern. From full ahead at $29\frac{1}{2}$ knots to full astern at $4\frac{1}{2}$ knots in $8\frac{1}{2}$ minutes!

The hospital facilities on the *Queen Elizabeth 2* were the largest and most modern ever fitted into a commercial vessel. The team of doctors and nurses are

A scene of splendor as the majestic *Queen Elizabeth 2* slowly steams up the channel toward Southampton. Her lights are ablaze and a low cloud ceiling reflects them back onto the ship. The picture was taken from the *Nieuw Amsterdam* late on the evening of June 30, 1970, as the two passed "like ships in the night."

capable of handling virtually any situation. Sometimes their services are in demand from other ships, as was the case on a number of occasions during 1970.

The first such call was on June 26, 1970 when the *QE2* was on an eastbound passage from New York to Le Havre. A message was received from the 3,514-ton German motor vessel *Zosmarr*, on a westbound passage to Boston, requesting medical advice for a sick Spanish seaman, Jesus Ferreira. Radio contact was established with the master of the *Zosmarr*, and the *QE2*'s principal medical officer, Dr. W. E. Deely, after hearing details of the illness, decided that the seaman's life could be in danger. The position of the *Zosmarr* was plotted, and a course was set to rendezvous with her. It was calculated that the *QE2* should meet the *Zosmarr* shortly after midnight. At 2000 hours Captain William J. Law gave the order to steer the new course to close with the German ship, which was instructed to steer a reciprocal course. While making for the rendezvous the *QE2* encountered dense fog, and her high-definition radars remained constantly manned as they scanned ahead. At 2345 the radars picked up the *Zosmarr* eighteen miles away, exactly on schedule. Contact was again made with the *Zosmarr* to give her instructions to enable the ships to maneuver together as close as possible. At 0025 hours the engines were stopped, and shortly after, one of the ship's boats was lowered into the sea and sent away with a doctor on board. Because of the dense fog and the pitch darkness, the *QE2* had to guide her launch across to the German ship. This was accomplished by the officer of the watch looking at a radar screen and giving instructions to the launch by walkie-talkie radio. The *Zosmarr* assisted by blowing her whistle periodically, and the launch sighted the little freighter at 0109 hours and soon thereafter went alongside. Fortunately, there was only a slight swell, and the sick seamen was able to descend to the *QE2*'s launch by climbing down the pilot ladder. The launch sped back to the liner, was hoisted aboard, and by 0126 hours the *Queen Elizabeth 2* had resumed her voyage to Le Havre at full speed. Following treatment, Jesus Ferreira made a full recovery.

Under similar circumstances, assistance was also rendered to seaman K. Hopner from the trawler *Heinrich Kern* on July 27, 1970, while the ships were in mid-Atlantic.

On October 29, 1970, on passage from Las Palmas to Dakar, the *Queen Elizabeth 2* diverted from course at 1236 hours to render assistance to an engineer officer injured on the S. S. *Cerinthus* of the Hadley Shipping Company, London. The fifth engineer, David R. G. Senior, had suffered second-degree burns on his hands and face and was in critical need of expert medical assistance. The *Queen* reached the Cerinthus at 1332 hours and the lifeboat was away by 1350, returning with the patient by 1422 hours, after which the *QE2* resumed full speed and the lucky man received the medical care his wounds required.

In June 1970 the *Queen* made her fastest crossing to date, covering the distance from Cóbh to New York in three days, twenty hours, forty minutes, at an average speed of 30.36 knots. Her reputation was growing. Evidence of the success of the *Queen Elizabeth 2* was on the eastbound crossing of July 23, 1970, when she carried her 75,000th passenger, who was presented with a plaque to commemorate the occasion.

Sir Basil Smallpeice, chairman of Cunard (1965–1971), presents to Douglas Ridley, chief officer and president of the officers' wardroom, the picture of Her Majesty Queen Elizabeth II that was a gift of the Queen to the ship in 1970. Looking on from the right is Commodore William Warwick, master of the *QE2*, and to the left is Captain Mortimer Hehir. Warwick, Hehir, and Ridley were all masters of the ship.

The French liner *Antilles* (1952, 19,828 tons, 599 feet by 80 feet). (Photo courtesy of the John H. Shaum, Jr. Collection.)

In October 1970 the *Queen Elizabeth 2* received a royal present of her own when Her Majesty Queen Elizabeth II presented portraits of herself and of Prince Philip to the officers' wardroom. The presentation at Southampton was made by Sir Basil Smallpeice on behalf of Her Majesty to the wardroom president, Chief Officer T. D. Ridley.

Cunard's earlier decision to order additional passenger liners resulted in a partnership with Overseas National Airlines, which had ordered a 17,000-ton cruise ship from the Rotterdam Drydock Company. This arrangement resulted in Cunard being able to take delivery of a new ship by the summer of 1971 and a second vessel a year later. On July 15, 1970, the announcement was made that the line had acquired 100 percent ownership of the new vessels from ONA and that they would be operated exclusively by Cunard. Sir Basil Smallpeice, commenting on the decision, said: "It underlines Cunard's determination to reestablish a modern and profitable passenger fleet at an early date." In November 1970 it was announced that the first of the new 17,000-ton liners would be named *Cunard Adventurer* in line with the emphasis on the company's cruise and leisure aspects of the 700 passenger vessels.

One of the most dramatic experiences of the *Queen Elizabeth 2* happened during the night of January 8–9, 1971. The giant Cunarder under the command of Commodore W. E Warwick was anchored off Castries, St. Lucia, on a Caribbean cruise when an S.O.S. was received from the French liner *Antilles* stating that she had run aground and was on fire near the island of Mustique in the Grenadines. The distress signal was received at 1905 hours and it was possible for the *QE2* to respond quickly, as she was already preparing to sail for her next port of call. By 1954 hours the *Queen* had weighed anchor and was steaming at full speed to the rescue. In the meantime, all departments on board were alerted to prepare for 500 survivors. Launch crews were mustered, gangway and scrambling nets were prepared, and volunteer parties of the *QE2* Scuba Divers' Club stood by. The hospital was on the alert and in the hotel department chefs and waiters stood by to prepare and serve food and drink. Blankets were made available, cabins prepared, and a reception desk was set up near the gangway to allocate them to the survivors as they came aboard. A list was made of those passengers with special skills who offered their services and of those who volunteered to give up their cabins to any needy survivor. Since the *Queen* had only approximately 1,000 passengers on board for the cruise, she had sufficient staterooms to accommodate the majority of the survivors without inconveniencing many of her own.

Three and a half hours after sailing from St. Lucia the *Queen Elizabeth 2* reached the search area. As she approached Mustique, the *Antilles* could be seen as a glow on the horizon, ablaze from stem to stern. The passengers on the *QE2* had a clear view of the *Antilles* as the *Queen* passed within a quarter of a mile of the stricken liner vividly marking the treacherous reef. Later, as more information became known, it appeared the desire had been to show the French liner's cruise passengers the beautiful sight of the island of Mustique against a Caribbean sunset. When the *Antilles* struck the uncharted reef, the impact caused fuel tanks to split open. Oil leaked into the engine room and soon became ignited, and attempts to contain the fire failed as it easily spread over the water in the flooded compartments. Passengers were ordered to their lifeboat stations. When the abandon ship order was given they proceeded ashore in lifeboats to the islands of Mustique and Bequia. The master and some of the crew remained on board in an unsuccessful attempt to fight the fire.

The *Queen Elizabeth 2* spent one hour in the search area near the burning inferno of the French liner and then sailed to Grand Bay, Mustique, to take on survivors who had already been transferred there by lifeboats. At Mustique, the darkness and a heavy swell made the transferring of survivors from the shore to the *QE2* difficult. Nevertheless, throughout the night, the *QE2*'s launches moved back and forth between the island and the ship with the *Antilles*. By 0505 hours on January 9 Commodore Warwick was able to assure the French Line at Fort de France, Martinique, that everyone had been accounted for from the *Antilles*. Unfortunately, however, the French liner was a total loss. Having taken all on board from Mustique, the *QE2* sailed for Barbados, where French Line agents had commenced preparations to receive the survivors. By the time the *Queen Elizabeth 2* arrived at Barbados the wind was too strong for her to go alongside in the harbor, so she anchored in the bay off

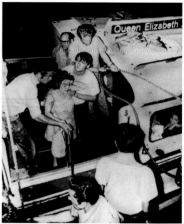

During the night of January 8–9, 1971, survivors of the French Line's *Antilles* board the *QE2* from her launches after being transported from the island of Mustique, following the wrecking and burning of the French liner on an uncharted reef.

Bridgetown. To assist with the ferrying of passengers and survivors ashore, seamen and launches from the *Carmania*, which was also in port, were seconded to the *QE2* as most of her crew had been on duty all through the night.

French Line officials boarded soon after arrival to arrange for the care and transportation of all those who desired it. Eighty-five passengers elected to remain on the *Queen* for a portion of her Caribbean cruise.

Congratulatory messages soon began to flood into the radio room of the *Queen Elizabeth 2*. Michael Noble, British minister for trade, on an official visit to Venezuela, sent the following to Commodore Warwick:

> I have much pleasure in sending you and all your officers, staff, crew and passengers hearty congratulations on your magnificent achievement in coming to the rescue of the passengers and crew of the S. S. *Antilles*. This was in the best traditions of British seamanship. I am glad that my presence in Venezuela makes it possible for me to send you these congratulations direct.

Similar messages were received from the United States Coast Guard in San Juan, the president of the French Line and Sir Basil Smallpeice in London.

The remainder of the 1970–1971 winter Caribbean cruise was relatively uneventful except for another mercy mission on March 15. En route from New York to Aruba, the ship aided a seaman who had fallen from the mast of the Norwegian vessel *Besna*. A launch was sent across from the *QE2* to collect the seaman, who subsequently recovered from his injuries.

The highlight of the early spring 1971 season was the maiden arrival of the *Queen Elizabeth 2* at Bermuda on March 26, 1971. Maiden arrivals always generate enthusiasm, but Bermuda has a special place in the hearts of many North Americans, and the Bermudians reciprocate these warm emotions where cruise ships and American and Canadian tourists are concerned.

The *QE2* had to anchor in the Great Sound as she was too large to dock in Hamilton.

Unfortunately, the financial situation of the Cunard Line deteriorated substantially during 1970 as a result of soaring costs. In Britain the president of the chamber of shipping noted increases in supplies and in costs of operation at a pace far greater than for a generation or more. Prices of fuel oil for ships increased by between 80 and 100 percent within one year, and other costs, such as seafarers' salaries and wages, port charges, and baggage and cargo handling, increased between 17 and 41 percent in a similar period. A total loss of £1.9 million pounds was declared, which also included Cunard's associated companies.

The presence of an economic recession in the United States and a strong U.S. government publicity campaign aimed at encouraging Americans to stay at home had not helped Cunard revenues. However, the outlook for the *QE2* in 1971 appeared more promising, with cruise bookings up 10 percent from the year before.

CHAPTER FOUR

Trafalgar House, Cunard, and the *QE2*

The summer of 1971 saw a fundamental change in the ownership of the Cunard Steam-Ship Company Limited. Cunard, after an independent existence of one hundred and thirty-two years, was the object of a successful takeover bid by the British company Trafalgar House Investments Ltd. For some weeks Cunard shares had been rising on the London Stock Exchange, a clear indication of a takeover bid when a company has not announced any great profits or new endeavors to warrant optimism. News articles involved a number of potential suitors during the month of June, and Cunard was forced to acknowledge that negotiations were under way with an undisclosed party.

Trafalgar House was interested in the Cunard Line as it complemented their hotel and leisure interests. The acquisition also offered substantial tax advantages. Trafalgar House had a 10 percent holding in Cunard, which was the maximum allowed before the public disclosure of interest was required. They also knew that another company, Slater, Walker Securities, held 11.6 percent, so they arranged for brokers to obtain them on their behalf. On June 30, 1971, Nigel Broakes, the chairman of Trafalgar House, informed Sir Basil Smallpeice that they now had a holding of over 21 percent in Cunard and that they were going to make a bid for the shipping line.

The initial £24 million offer made by Trafalgar was met with resistance by Cunard and some of the shareholders, but this was overcome when the value of the company was increased to £27.3 million.

In a message to Cunard Line employees, the chairman stated that the Trafalgar House bid was accepted because "Cunard Line have now received all the assurances they requested from Trafalgar about Cunard's future role in

The *Queen* glides through the calm waters of the majestic Geiranger Fjord in Norway on her celebrated North Cape cruise.

the British shipping industry." In addition, it was stated: "Trafalgar House have given assurances that if their bid is successful Cunard will remain as a shipping company within the Trafalgar Group and will continue as a major force in the British shipping industry and also that *QE2* will continue to operate under the British flag." Sir Basil Smallpeice closed by asking "all Cunard staff afloat and ashore to continue unabated their efforts to ensure the company's future prosperity and their own place within it wherever the future ownership of the company's shares may lie."

On August 26, 1971, Victor Matthews of Trafalgar House Investments Ltd. took over as the chairman of the Cunard Steamship Company Ltd.

The *Queen Elizabeth 2* was acknowledged by the new owners as a potential money maker, and the orders that Cunard had placed for new tonnage were praised, even if some of the existing assets of the company did not appear so financially attractive—notably the *Carmania* and *Franconia*, both of which Cunard had been trying to sell. The new management of Cunard announced the withdrawal from service of the two ships in October 1971 and their subsequent lay-up awaiting sale.

During the summer season of 1971, the *Queen Elizabeth 2* continued to

The transportation of passengers' cars can be a major drawing card for the *Queen*. Depending upon the facilities available and the nature of the tide, cars can be driven on through one of the nine shell doors in the sides of the ship, or lifted on by derrick and lowered through the hatch.

carry the rich and the famous across the Atlantic. Mr. and Mrs. Blake Edwards and Mr. and Mrs. Michael S. Laughlin crossed in July, Mrs. Edwards being better known as Julie Andrews and Mrs. Laughlin as Leslie Caron—both famous members of the theatrical world. The holds of the *Queen* accommodate automobiles and frequently have been occupied by vintage machines, stately limousines, and racing cars. Mr. Robin Ormes, the motor racing ace, shipped his Lola to participate in the Watkins Glen Six-Hour International Sports Car Race on July 24, 1971.

On passage from Cóbh to New York the *QE2* received a request for medical assistance from the ocean weather ship *Charlie*. The call was received at 1959 hours on September 12, and the liner altered course to reach the rendezvous at 2030 hours. At 0027 hours in pitch darkness the *Queen* hove to and the United States Coast Guard cutter *Chase* transferred the seaman to the liner. Eighteen minutes later she proceeded on her way to New York.

Cunard's association with the port of Boston goes back to the inception of transatlantic service in 1840. There has always been a warm and close regard between the people of New England and the line, and the maiden arrival of the *Queen Elizabeth 2* in Boston caused quite a stir. The *Queen* stopped en route from New York to Le Havre on October 1, 1971, to embark approximately 300 members of the Honorable Artillery Company of Massachusetts. Created in 1638, the organization was the first military company chartered in the Western Hemisphere, and it has been in continuous existence ever since. In 1971 they decided to cross the ocean on the *Queen Elizabeth 2* to have their 334th Field Day Tour of Duty in England. The liner was suitably dressed for the occasion, with all flags flying as an armada of small craft greeted her. The official welcoming ceremonies included the presentation of a Cunard flag to

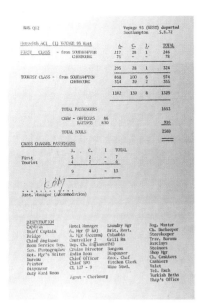

The Souls Sheet provides the fundamental breakdown of passengers, officers, and crew for any voyage. The enormous carrying capacity of the *Queen Elizabeth 2* is dramatically underlined with the simple figures: passengers, 1,653; officers, 86; crew, 830; total souls = 2,569. Furthermore, while Voyage No. 93 (west) in August 1972 was well booked, she could, if necessary, accommodate nearly 400 additional passengers and almost another 100 crew.

the city of Boston. In full dress uniform, the Ancient Honorable Artillery Company marched from Fanueil Hall to Commonwealth Pier, where they were welcomed on board the *Queen*.

R. B. Patton, president of Cunard, fitted his comments to the jocular nature of the occasion when he said, "I also want to thank Commodore Warwick for his hospitality this morning. At this hour, the British often enjoy a different sort of beverage, but ever since another party on board a British ship got a little out of hand, we've made it a rule to put the tea under guard while in Boston Harbor. But this is truly an occasion that calls for champagne—to describe it in appropriate terms, the greatest ship in the world has come to the hub of the universe." Patton concluded: "To the Ancient and Honorable Artillery Company, welcome aboard and bon voyage; you honor us by choosing our ship. We're proud and happy to have such a distinguished send-off on our first sailing."

In the first six months of their ownership, Trafalgar House undertook a complete survey of the *Queen Elizabeth 2* and the services she could provide. It was decided that £1 million would be spent on improvements to the ship. These included modifications to the restaurants and the construction and installation of the luxury penthouse suites on the Signal and Sports Decks.

The 1972 season on the North Atlantic was made interesting by at least one violent storm and the presence of an enormous amount of ice in the steamer lanes. Captain Mortimer Hehir commanded the *Queen* on a memorable crossing on April 16–23, 1972, when a violent storm raged across the North Atlantic for 1,500 miles, with 50-foot seas and 100-mile-an-hour winds. The horrendous conditions continued for four days. At times when one looked around there was nothing to be seen but spume and spray in all directions.

A major transformation of the external appearance of the *Queen* occurred in 1972 with the addition of ten penthouse suites on the Sports Deck slightly behind the mast. The prefabricated suites were lifted on board at Southampton during the annual refit at Vosper Thornycroft in the fall.

The addition of the penthouse suites gave the *QE2* additional superlative accommodations, which are very popular. The preparations on the ship and the prefabrication of the units at Vosper Thornycroft had to be technically exact for the pieces to fit.

The actors Robert Wagner and Natalie Wood were passengers and described the storm on the *Queen* as "a great experience—it was very exciting." On arrival at Southampton certificates were passed out to the passengers who had "survived" the worst storm in memory.

Certainly one of the most bizarre crossings the *Queen Elizabeth 2* experienced began when the liner sailed from New York on Monday, May 15, 1972, under the command of Captain William J. Law. In mid-Atlantic on Wednesday evening, May 17, the captain received a coded message from the New York office of Cunard Line vice-president Charles Dickson to the effect that an anonymous caller had threatened a bomb explosion on board the 65,000-ton liner and demanded ransom. The threat had been made known to Cunard in New York, and it was confirmed from London that there might be two accomplices traveling on the ship. Captain Law initiated every possible security arrangement in cooperation with his senior officers, and a discreet search was carried out. Nothing was found.

The Ministry of Defence in London was alerted and plans made to send bomb disposal experts out to board the *QE2* in mid-Atlantic. Captain Law made the following announcement to passengers at 1600 hours on Thursday, May 18:

Ladies and gentlemen, we have received information concerning a threat of a bomb explosion on board this ship some time during this voyage. We have received such threats in the past which have so far turned out to be hoaxes. However, we always take them seriously and take every possible precaution.

On this occasion we are being assisted by the British government who are sending out bomb disposal experts who will be parachuted into the sea and picked up by boat and brought aboard.

I will of course keep you fully informed about the situation. Cunard are taking every precaution ashore and on board and will take any necessary action to minimize risk. If there is any question of it being necessary to pay over money this will be done ashore in New York.

I can only ask you to remain calm. On these occasions lots of rumors tend to circulate. Please only take notice of any information that comes from me directly or from one of my officers. That is all for the moment.

At 1636 hours the *Queen* began to reduce speed prior to rendezvousing with an R.A.F. Nimrod (jet reconnaissance aircraft) from St. Mawgan's in Cornwall in a position 740 miles due east of Cape Race, Newfoundland. The Nimrod was in sight at 1706 hours, positioning was verified, communication established, and the *QE2* slowed to a stop at 1734 hours in a position 45.8 degrees north and 35.1 degrees west. A little less than half an hour later, at 1808 hours, an R.A.F. Hercules was sighted carrying the four members of the bomb disposal team. Crews for two of the *QE2*'s launches were standing by, and one was immediately lowered, with First Officer Robin A. Woodall in charge, accompanied by Second Officer Ronald W. Warwick. As the *QE2* and the launch headed into the wind, the pilot of the Hercules made a few preliminary runs to decide on the best approach. In addition to the weather being dull and miserable, the situation was further complicated by the fact that the height of cloud base was approximately 400 feet above sea level, which was too low for a safe parachute jump to be made. It was therefore necessary for the pilot to bring his plane in below the cloud level, sight the launch, and then climb quickly up through the clouds to about 800 feet. A few seconds later, although it seemed like an eternity, the first two parachutes drifted down out of the clouds. Two such runs were made, releasing two parachutists at a time and dropping them with great precision near the *QE2*'s launch. The *Queen*'s experienced boat crew had all four parachutists in the launch within five minutes of them landing in the water. The bomb disposal experts wore frogman suits and carried a considerable amount of equipment and, as a special consideration, a London newspaper for the captain. Most of the passengers were on deck to

Comparisons of the *Queen Elizabeth 2* with other vessels are difficult to envision, but in this scene of the old and the new, the Portuguese tall ship *Sagres* is shown passing the *Queen*.

view the splashdowns and cheered the successful proceedings. It would have been difficult not to have been thrilled by the operation and the courage of the individuals concerned. The Hercules turned back eastwards to her base in England some 1,380 miles away, but the Nimrod stayed around until the ship's launch was safely aboard the liner. She then bade the *Queen* farewell and returned to Cornwall. The *Queen Elizabeth 2* was under way again at 1924 hours.

As the entertainment for the evening commenced, the bomb disposal experts began a systematic search of the ship from stem to stern. Those courageous gentlemen were Captain Robert Williams and Sergeant Clifford Oliver of the Royal Ordnance Corps and Lieutenant Richard Clifford and Corporal Thomas Jones of the Royal Marine amphibious training unit at Poole. No explosive devices of any nature were ever discovered, and the *QE2* safely arrived at Cherbourg and Southampton with her passengers and crew.

In New York the scene had been one of considerable tension for Charles Dickson, who had received the anonymous telephone call about the supposed bomb and the ransom demand. The caller appeared to know what he was talking about and commented that, while he and his compatriots had considered asking for $1 million, they had settled on a ransom of $350,000 in exchange for not blowing the ship up. The caller refused to say when he would call back, so the Cunard office telephones were manned day and night. In London, the chairman of Cunard Line, Victor Matthews, was alerted in the middle of the night and agreed to the ransom payment, which was assembled in New York and placed in a briefcase for delivery when so ordered. No one ever appeared to collect the money.

The American police and the Federal Bureau of Investigation worked day and night on the case but remained in the background until the *QE2* safely reached Europe. Ultimately a man from New York was arrested and charged with extortion. He was tried in Manhattan Federal Court, found guilty, and sentenced to twenty years.

An unfortunate result of the bomb threat with all its ramifications was that Cunard decided no longer to permit unrestricted access to the liner for the general public or for individuals seeing passengers off. Accordingly, the long-standing tradition of the on-board bon-voyage party was canceled and future passengers would have to bid their fond farewells on the pier.

During the spring of 1972 reports were received from the United States and Canadian meteorological offices that there was a large area of ice south of Newfoundland. The ice, drifting from the Labrador Basin, had not traveled so far south for over thirty years. Because of the warnings, the *QE2* had to take a course 100 miles to the south of her usual route.

On passage from Cherbourg to New York during the small hours of August 21, 1972, the *Queen Elizabeth 2* reduced speed to rendezvous with the U.S. Coast Guard Cutter *Hamilton*, which was being used as an ocean weather observing station known as *Delta*. One of her seamen, W. D. Emmett, had received word that a member of his family was critically ill, and an inquiry had been made if there was any possibility of assistance from the *Queen Elizabeth 2*.

The Gare Maritime at Cherbourg plays host to the *Queen Elizabeth 2* on a number of occasions each year. Originally built to accommodate the *Queen Mary* and the *Queen Elizabeth*, the French terminal is the only remaining one the *QE2* uses regularly that served the older *Queens*. The giant passageways descend to meet the appropriate doors on the side of the liner.

A launch was sent over from the other ship, and within eight minutes of her being alongside the *QE2* had ordered full speed ahead for her destination.

Toward the end of 1972, prosperity in the shipping division was underlined when Trafalgar House announced plans to build another cruise liner. During the naming ceremony of the *Cunard Ambassador* at Rotterdam on October 21, 1972, Victor Matthews said the hull and engines of the new liner would be built by Burmeister Wein of Copenhagen and the fitting out would be accomplished in Italy by INMA of La Spezia because three British yards had declined to tender for the contract. The order for a sister ship was placed in January 1973. The two ships entered service as the *Cunard Countess* and the *Cunard Princess*.

Among the more interesting and exciting experiences that the *Queen Elizabeth 2* faced in 1973 were two Silver Anniversary Cruises to Israel, under the auspices of Assured Travel Services, Inc., of Massachusetts, designed to cover the Passover/Easter holiday (April 14–28, 1973) and the twenty-fifth anniversary celebrations for Israel (April 28–May 13, 1973). They attracted a considerable amount of publicity, as it was thought by many that the *QE2* was vulnerable to an attack by Arab terrorists. As a result of these fears, and in consultation with the British Ministry of Defence, strict security measures were taken throughout the cruise.

When the *QE2* arrived at Southampton from her Caribbean cruise on April 12, 1973, the Southampton Ocean Terminal was sealed off from the public and armed guards went aboard. Meanwhile, Royal Naval skin divers kept vigil over the underwater hull of the *Queen* as she took on stores and awaited her passengers.

The *Queen* sailed from Southampton with only about 600 passengers, less than a third of her capacity, and returned from Israel on the second cruise with approximately the same number. Certainly adverse publicity and heightened security concern took their toll on the bookings. For those who did make the cruise to Israel, or back, there was a fabulous opportunity to enjoy the ship and be pampered with a crew-to-passenger ratio of two to one.

Special arrangements were made to provide a complete kosher service for the large percentage of Jewish passengers. The entire Columbia kitchen and restaurant* were made kosher for the cruise, conforming with the highest standards of kashruth.

First stop on the cruise itinerary was a call at Lisbon, Portugal, on April 17, 1973. Portuguese authorities were very concerned about security and even went so far as to halt all traffic on the giant suspension bridge spanning the Tagus River while the *Queen* passed beneath the soaring span. The Lisbon

*Now named Caronia.

A scene of awesome power and majesty: the *Queen Elizabeth 2* slices through North Atlantic swells during a crossing in August 1972. The penthouses have not been added yet, although work on them is underway; hence the *Queen* looks much as her original designers intended—sleek, modern, and powerful.

passenger terminal was closed to all visitors, and passengers were searched before being permitted to rejoin the ship if they went ashore. After leaving Lisbon the *Queen* set course for Israel. The ship was under orders to complete the voyage to Israel at her maximum speed and to extinguish all unnecessary external lights. Her arrival on April 21 marked the inaugural visit of the *QE2* to Israel and a unique occasion for the town of Ashdod—the first-ever visit of a passenger liner to the port. Ashdod is a convenient departure point for land tours to Jerusalem, which is only forty-four miles away, and other points of interest. The liner stayed four days at Ashdod and then proceeded to Haifa for a similar period. While in Haifa, the former Prime Minister of Israel, David Ben-Gurion visited the ship.

A major event on any world cruise is the arrival in Hong Kong. The point of origin for many land tours to the People's Republic of China; Hong Kong also is a picturesque tourist center and a fabulous marketplace all of its own.

On April 29 the passengers from the Easter/Passover cruise flew home and the passengers for the Silver Independence Day Cruise joined the ship for a reversal of the itinerary until the *QE2* sailed from Ashdod on May 8 for the return voyage to Southampton via Palma de Mallorca. The liner returned safely to Britain on May 13, 1973, without incident.

Over a year later, on July 16, 1974, President Anwar Sadat of Egypt revealed in a BBC television interview with Lord Chalfont, former minister of state at the Foreign and Commonwealth Office, that he personally had countermanded an order given to an Egyptian submarine commander by an Arab leader to torpedo the *Queen Elizabeth 2* during her cruise to Israel.

The future for the *Queen Elizabeth 2* brightened with the announcement that the liner would sail on her first world cruise on January 4, 1975, a ninety-two-day odyssey through the Panama Canal and around the world. The cruise from Southampton to Southampton would cover over 38,000 miles and take the *Queen* on an easterly course to more than twenty major ports around the globe. Norman Thompson, Cunard's managing director at the time, told the press: "We think *QE2* is the best ship afloat for this type of cruise." A long cruise has been made annually ever since.

The *QE2* returned to the North Atlantic for 1973 with high hopes for her most successful season ever. Americans were preparing to travel more as the recession lessened and business conditions improved.

This was Captain William Law's last season as master of the *Queen*. He relinquished his command on August 5, 1973, after thirty-six years of service with the Cunard Line. Captain Mortimer F. Hehir was appointed master of the *QE2* in his place. Captain Peter Jackson became staff captain and relieving master of the *Queen*.

An unusual voyage made by the *Queen Elizabeth 2* was in the summer of 1973 when the ship was chartered for a cruise to Come by Chance, Newfoundland, in honor of the opening of the new oil refinery on the shores of Placentia Bay. The liner docked at the pier of the Newfoundland Refining Company, which soon would be hosting supertankers transporting the products from the 100,000-barrel-a-day refinery. John M. Shaheen, chairman of NRC, said, "Chartering the *QE2* allowed us to give everybody a first-hand look at the year-round, deep-water, docking facilities available in Placentia Bay, which is one of the major reasons for locating the refinery at Come By Chance." The invited guests aboard the *Queen* included representatives from major oil, financial, shipping, engineering, and construction interests.

The winter of 1973 brought a three-day cruise from New York to chase the comet Kohoutek, expected to be one of the brightest comets of the twentieth century. The cruise was completely sold out when the *Queen* sailed from New York on December 9 on the "comet watch." Guest of honor on board the liner was the Czech-born astronomer Professor Lubos Kohoutek, who first identified the comet in March 1973 and predicted its brilliance. Dr. Isaac Asimov, the science fiction writer, was also booked as part of the enrichment program for the cruise. Unfortunately, the weather did not provide much respite from overcast conditions and rain, which made chasing the comet futile. Later Caribbean cruises were blessed with clear air and balmy weather, which permitted passengers to see the comet.

The biggest headache that the Cunard Line faced in the mid-1970s was the enormous increase in the cost of bunkering oil, which went up from $20 to $70 a ton. Some critics complained that the *Queen* represented a poor use of a scarce resource. In a letter to the London Times, this argument was forcefully met by Norman S. Thompson, managing director of Cunard, who noted that the fuel consumption of the *QE2* over a 3,060-mile transatlantic voyage at a speed of 28 $\frac{1}{2}$ knots was approximately 1.55 tons per individual when she was carrying 1,500 passengers—relatively efficient in comparison with comparable vessels.

One activity that could generate good publicity and profit for the *QE2* was to use the ship as a venue while in port. When the election campaign committee for New York Mayor Abraham Beame was casting around for a means of reducing the debt for the mayoralty campaign, they decided to hold a birthday

Entering New York at the end of an Atlantic run, the bow of the *Queen Elizabeth 2* is highlighted by the early morning sun. She has just cleared the Verrazano Narrows Bridge, and seasoned travelers may just be stirring from their beds while those who have not experienced an arrival by sea in New York Harbor will have been up for some time to see the sights.

party for His Honor on the *Queen* on the evening of March 21, 1974. Tickets for the novel function sold at $250 a head to 1,000 of Mayor and Mrs. Beame's closest friends. To make the whole thing more realistic, guests were given regular cruise tickets and "embarked" as though they were about to sail. The ship became the scene of a very lively party and a spectacular salute to one of New York City's leaders.

The *Queen Elizabeth 2* appeared to be sailing toward a £2,000,000 profit for the 1973–1974 fiscal year when she encountered misfortune. She was steaming some 200 miles off Bermuda at around 0400 hours on April 1, 1974, when the alarm on an electronic probe designed to detect the presence of oil or other contaminants in the pure water of her boilers failed. The boilers consist of an arrangement of hundreds of pipes through which the water passes. A film of oil spread through some of these, and the furnace, instead of heating the water inside the tubes, heated the tubes themselves and damaged them. The propulsion system was shut down immediately before any further damage occurred. The ship's engineers worked hard to rectify the fault, but as there was a chance that this would not be done in a reasonable time Cunard decided to leave nothing to chance and commenced making contingency plans. The president of Flagship Cruises in Oslo, Norway, was contacted and arrangements were made for the *Sea Venture*, which was on a three-day visit to Bermuda, to render assistance.

Captain Torbjorn Hauge, master of the *Sea Venture*, sailed his ship almost immediately for the *QE2*'s last position, leaving nearly four hundred of his own cruise passengers ashore. Two hundred and two passengers elected to stay with the officer and crew of the *Sea Venture* to experience the adventure and assist if possible. The Bermuda authorities assisted by providing hotel accommodations for the other Flagship Cruise passengers left behind until their ship returned. Meanwhile, Cunard chartered aircraft to meet the *QE2*'s passengers in Bermuda and to fly them back to the United States.

At sea the *QE2*'s passengers danced all night under the stars and regarded the whole experience as an adventure. Throughout their stay on board they were kept fully informed at regular intervals by the master, Captain Peter Jackson, over the public address system operated from the bridge. By doing this, the master undoubtedly contributed much to the well-being and peace of mind of the passengers and relieved them of any anxiety.

The *Sea Venture* reached the *Queen* at 0330 hours on April 3, and the plans for the transfer of the *QE2*'s passengers using the Norwegian ship's launches were formalized. The *Sea Venture* maneuvered as close as possible to the *Queen*, and the two ships between them provided a calm stretch of water for the transfer of the 1,654 passengers.

A thousand life jackets and twenty inflatable rubber rafts were sent over to the *Sea Venture* because with all the passengers from the *QE2* the Norwegian liner would be way over her normal complement. Disembarkation took place from two gangways on Five Deck. The first launch departed with passengers at 0805 hours, and by 1539 hours they had all disembarked. The discharge of baggage followed, and a little over two hours later the whole operation was concluded and the *Sea Venture* set her course for Hamilton.

The crew of the *Sea Venture* found accommodations for 700 in cabins, and the remainder were provided with blankets and deckchairs or portable beds in the public rooms.

An all-night buffet and free bar service was provided on the *Sea Venture* throughout the overnight trip. Most of the passengers who were taken off the *QE2* gave her officers and crew high marks and were delighted with the services and total refund of their fares made by Cunard. The incident certainly ranks as one of the most difficult experiences the *Queen* has ever faced, but the prompt, efficient manner in which all aspects of the problem were handled redounded substantially to the good will of the line. Many passengers said that they hoped to travel again with Cunard in the near future.

When the tug arrived from New York, the *QE2* was towed to Bermuda, where preliminary repairs were carried out. She then sailed at reduced speed to New York, where they were completed.

The launches of the *QE2* do yeoman's duty carrying passengers back and forth from the ship into ports where she cannot berth. Designated units also serve as rescue vessels when called upon, while all, collectively, ensure the safety of the *Queen's* passengers and crew.

The towering side of the *Queen Elizabeth 2* stretches to the heavens in the view of passengers departing from the *Queen* by launch.

Captain Peter Jackson and the officers and crew of the *Queen Elizabeth 2* received a special radiogram from Victor Matthews, managing director of the Cunard Line:

> The following motion has been tabled in the House of Commons today by Mr. Robert Taylor, conservative member of Parliament for North West Croydon which speaks for itself. That this house congratulates the management of Cunard for the exemplary manner in which it discharged every possible legal and moral obligation to the passengers of the *QE2* during the recent voyage and considers that in doing so it has maintained the highest reputation of British commerce.

Mr. Matthews commented that it was understood to be quite rare for a commercial organization to be so recognized in the House. He stated: "As your Chairman I would like to thank each and every one of you who have played a part in bringing this about. The strength of a team can only be judged in adverse conditions and I would particularly like to congratulate the Captain, officers and crew for their magnificent performance."

The *Queen* sailed on schedule from New York on Tuesday, April 16, 1974, on her first transatlantic crossing for the season. On the way across Cunard and Dunhill sponsored the world's first backgammon tournament played aboard a liner. Players included Earl Lichfield, Liberal M.P. Clement Freud, and comedian Spike Milligan. The tournament was won by Mr. Charles Benson, who collected £10,000 in prize money.

On April 25, 1974, the *QE2* sailed on a twelve-day cruise with 1,540 passengers to the Mediterranean. When she departed she was given a farewell salute by the British army helicopter display team, the Blue Eagles.

At Cannes a rare event occurred when the *Queen Elizabeth 2* and the *France* anchored near each other for a day, and onlookers from shore could observe the two largest liners in the world. It had already been announced by the French government that the *France* was to be withdrawn at the end of the 1974 season as an economy measure, since the liner's deficit of $12 million a year had ballooned with the inflation in fuel prices. Accordingly, Cunard announced that the *QE2* would increase the number of North Atlantic crossings to thirty-one for the 1975 season in a partial attempt to fill the gap and to benefit from being the only remaining transatlantic superliner.

On rare occasions, a New York Harbor pilot may get a longer ride than he bargained for when he takes a vessel to sea. Normally the pilot is dropped near the Ambrose Light, but on August 25, 1974, pilot John Cahill found himself a guest of the Cunard Line for an Atlantic crossing when the pilot cutter was engaged in a rescue mission and could not take him off. Accordingly, he enjoyed a five-day ocean crossing to Southampton and a free trip back by air with all the trimmings accorded to fare-paying passenger.

Later, on September 25, 1974, while on passage from Naples to Barcelona, the eternal watchfulness of the Cunard officers on the bridge paid off handsomely for some distressed yachtsmen. The *Queen Elizabeth 2* was steaming through gale-force winds and a rough Mediterranean Sea when at 0215 hours red

distress flares were sighted to the north. The *Queen* immediately answered so peremptory a summons of the sea and altered course through the heavy seas and the darkness to investigate. Fifteen minutes later, at 0230 hours, a small yacht in severe difficulty was sighted. The individuals on the yacht were incapable of doing anything, so the 963-foot *QE2* had to maneuver on her two engines in the gale conditions. Six male survivors of the yacht *Stephanie* of Toulon were rescued by 0345 hours, and the *Queen* resumed passage to Barcelona. The fickleness of the sea takes some and leaves others to be rescued by a vessel beyond their wildest dreams.

CHAPTER FIVE

Cruising the World

When the *Queen* sailed from Southampton on January 4, 1975, under the command of Captain Mortimer Hehir, she set out on her maiden world cruise. She left England with 342 passengers and picked up another 570 in New York and additional passengers in Port Everglades, Florida. At various ports around the world other passengers joined or left the ship. Everywhere she went, the *Queen* was given a royal reception—from Cape Town to Singapore, Hong Kong to Kobe, Honolulu to Acapulco. One of the highlights of the world cruise was for 600 passengers to make an historic three-day excursion from Hong Kong into the People's Republic of China.

During the Pacific crossing a country fair was held on board to raise funds for charitable causes. The event is similar to those held each year during the summer months in towns and villages throughout England. The activities, to name a few, included raffles, tombola, a tug-of-war contest, fortune telling, a human fruit machine, and an auction for the navigator's world cruise chart. The fair has become an annual tradition on the *QE2* and over the years hundreds of thousands of dollars have been raised by passengers and crew.

The last leg of the world cruise, Los Angeles to New York via the Panama Canal, had a waiting list of over 300 people. When the *Queen* made her first transit of the canal in March 1975, she became the largest passenger ship in the world to do so—surpassing the record held by the German liner Bremen (51,731 tons) in 1936.

The six locks that comprise the mechanical portions of the Panama Canal are 110 feet wide by 1,000 feet long. The *Queen Elizabeth 2* is just over 105 feet wide and 963 feet long. As the *Queen* leaves the Pacific and steams past Balboa

The island of Tristan da Cunha issued one of the largest stamps in the world to honor the arrival of the *Queen Elizabeth 2* in one of her stops on a world cruise. Native vessels and the symbol of the Cunard Line, a gold lion rampant against a crimson background encircled by a golden rope, complete the design of the stamp.

toward the Miraflores locks, the impression is that she never will succeed in "threading the needle." Slowly but surely, the huge liner edges into the first of the three locks that will lift the ship 85 feet above the Pacific Ocean to the level of Gatun Lake. Once locked in with a clearance of less than 30 inches on each side, 26,000,000 gallons of water will begin to flow from Gatun Lake by gravity into the lock. A short passage through the Miraflores Lake takes the *QE2* to the Pedro Miguel locks, which raise the liner in another two steps to Gatun Lake, which spans the continent.

Several hours' steaming is necessary to cross the 30-mile-wide Gatun Lake and pass through the picturesque Gaillard Cut, where the canal was excavated through the mountains of the Continental Divide. A monument used to mark the Continental Divide as a memorial to those who lost their lives building the waterway, but it was recently removed when widening of the canal commenced. Once on the eastern side, the *Queen* enters the first of three locks that lower the ship to the level of the Atlantic Ocean.

The transit time of the Panama Canal is usually about eight hours but depends on the number and tonnage of ships scheduled. For passenger liners like the *QE2* who want to transit during daylight and for other vessels whose schedules are critical, an advanced reservation system is available at extra cost guaranteeing a fixed time and date for crossing the continent. The transit fees for the Panama Canal are based upon the tonnage of the vessel as calculated by the Canal Authority. When the *Queen Elizabeth 2* crossed the Isthmus for the first time, she set the record for paying the highest toll. Today the transit costs for the *QE2* are over $100,000.

By the time the *QE2* returned to England on April 6, 1975, over 3,965 people had been on board at some stage of the cruise, and she had steamed 39,470 miles in ninety-two days to twenty-four ports in nineteen countries across four continents.

All voyages on the *QE2* can be tailored to suit individual preferences and time parameters. Today's marketing, aided by the speed of jet aircraft, makes it possible for passengers to experience the whole of a world cruise or to enjoy sections of the cruise with air service to and from the *Queen* wherever she may be.

Traditionally, the year-long schedule of the *Queen Elizabeth 2* begins with the first Atlantic crossing of the regular season around the middle of April. Those who do not care to fly will arrange their departure from Europe or the United States to coincide with the first sailing. By planning a schedule of approximately twenty-five to thirty Atlantic crossings each season, the *Queen* succeeds in maintaining her position on the North Atlantic as the last of the great ocean liners and heiress to a tradition of service spanning nearly one hundred and sixty years.

The provisioning of the *Queen Elizabeth 2* for crossings and cruising involves loading a variety of items at the main ports of Southampton and New York. Computerized systems accurately monitor the stock levels of stores and daily consumption. Provisioning is arranged many months in advance to ensure the best quality is obtained in the quantities required. The following list gives the average consumption of food for one week with 1,700 passengers on board:

Baby food	135 jars	Ice cream	865 gals.
Bacon	2,625 lbs.	Jam	525 lbs.
Beef	7,720 lbs.	Kippers	200 lbs.
Beer	4,780 cans, 18 brands	Lamb	1,005 lbs.
Biscuits	210 lbs.	Liqueurs	70 bottles, 26 types
Brandy	30 bottles, 12 brands	Lobster	1,950 lbs.
Butter	2,455 lbs.	Milk	1,600 gals.
Caviar	55 lbs.	Minerals	5,320 cans, 12 types
Champagne	1,160 bottles, 19 brands	Pork	1,100 lbs.
Cheese	1,275 lbs.	Port	15 bottles, 11 brands
Chicken	2,750 lbs.	Potatoes	6,700 lbs.
Coffee	600 lbs.	Prawns	595 lbs.
Cream	210 gals	Rum	15 bottles, 5 brands
Duck	1,300 lbs.	Sausages	1,840 lbs.
Eggs	2,342 doz.	Sherry	35 bottles, 6 brands
Flour	410 lbs.	Smoked salmon	485 lbs.
Foie gras	19 lbs.	Suckling pig	60 lbs.
Fresh Fruit	7,000 lbs.	Sugar	1,965 lbs.
Fresh vegetables	16,410 lbs.	Tea	26,500 bags
Fresh fish	2,010 lbs.	Turkey	990 lbs.
Frozen fish	995 lbs.	Venison	250 lbs.
Game hens	410	Vodka	70 bottles, 5 brands
Gin	55 bottles, 4 brands	Whiskey	155 bottles, 35 brands
Haggis	30 lbs.	Wine	2,200 bottles, 203 labels
Ham	795 lbs.		

The size of the *QE2* makes any transit of the canal an adventure; the maximum clearance is only 30 inches per side. The liner is 963 feet in length and the locks are 1,100 feet.

The *QE2* pays the highest toll of any vessel using the Panama Canal on the basis of her size and the nature of her "cargo" as a passenger ship. In the case of the *Queen* the fees exceed $90,000 per transit, but this is still a bargain compared to the cost of steaming 11,000 miles around South America. (Photo courtesy of David Barnicote.)

Between North Atlantic crossings, short cruises are sometimes made from Southampton to Spain, Portugal, and the Atlantic Islands. On the west side of the ocean, cruises are usually made from New York to Canada and Nova Scotia and to Bermuda or to the nearer Caribbean ports. Periodically the *Queen* will make a three-day cruise to "nowhere" from either New York or Southampton.

A popular midsummer sailing is the North Cape Cruise from Southampton to the "Land of the Midnight Sun" and the fjords of Norway. The North Cape Cruise nearly always features the natural magnificence of the Geiranger Fjord along with a visit to the land of the Lapps and reindeer and lasts between eight to twelve days. Because of the tremendously long and varied coastline of Norway, the *Queen* has visited sixteen different ports in that Scandinavian country since she was commissioned.

There is always a Caribbean cruise over Christmas and New Year. The ship is decorated from stem to stern for the holidays and a traditional festive atmosphere enables the year-end celebrations to be carried out in a tropical setting.

The *Queen*'s 1975 North Atlantic season proved relatively uneventful until June 20, when, on passage from Cherbourg to New York, she received a call at 2204 hours from the Russian trawler *Luga* (2,690 tons) asking for assis-

Twenty-six million gallons of fresh water from Gatun Lake supply the power through gravity flow to move the *Queen* through the locks. No pumps are necessary.

There are only inches to spare as the *Queen* slips into a lock. The electrically powered cog-railroad "mules" pull the huge liner through the locks in tandem.

tance for a sick seaman, Aleck Sungayala, of Latvia, who was ill with a suspected burst ulcer. The *QE2* altered course and steamed 128 miles to rendezvous with the factory ship, which was sighted at 0210 hours. By 0258 hours the sick seaman was on board the *Queen* and four minutes later she resumed her voyage to New York.

On December 4, 1975, while on passage between Antigua and Boston, the *Queen Elizabeth 2* completed her first million miles of steaming.

Further away in the Caribbean, Mrs. Neil Armstrong, wife of the astronaut and first man to step on the moon, was making maritime history when she became the first American woman to christen a Cunard Line passenger vessel. Following the ceremony at San Juan on August 8, 1976, the *Cunard Countess* put to sea on the first of many weekly Caribbean cruises.

On March 1, 1977, the company sold the *Cunard Adventurer* to a Norwegian company, and she was re-registered the *Southward II*. Soon afterward, on March 30, Her Serene Highness Princess Grace of Monaco christened the Cunard Line's latest cruise liner, the *Cunard Princess*, at a ceremony held in New York.

The schedule for 1977 involved the Jubilee World Cruise of ninety-two days and a series of European and Caribbean cruises in the spring and fall in-

The three Gatun locks on the Atlantic side are all together and are not divided like the Pacific trio. In any crossing from the Atlantic to the Pacific, passengers marvel at the wonders of the Panama Canal locks.

As the lock gates open, the *Queen* prepares to continue her voyage.

The *QE2* steams through the Gaillard Cut 85 feet above sea level and over the Continental Divide. Over 25,000 men lost their lives building the Panama Railroad (1849–1855) and then digging the Panama Canal (French effort, 1878–1888, and American effort, 1903–1914). (Photo courtesy of David Barnicote.)

terspliced with thirty Atlantic crossings. In London, Trafalgar House had bought the venerable Ritz Hotel and completely refurbished it to bring the great institution up to the standards of excellence for which its founder had been famous. The LaToc Hotel in St. Lucia and the Paradise Beach Hotel in Barbados continued to prove to be among the outstanding values in that re-

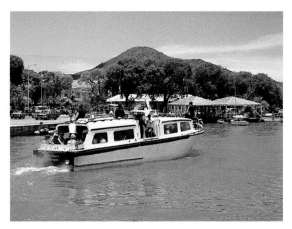

At the end of a full day, the *QE2*'s launch speeds away from the pier at Charlotte Amalie, St. Thomas, Virgin Islands, with another load of passengers returning to the ship.

Her Serene Highness Princess Grace of Monaco christens the new cruise ship *Cunard Princess* during a visit to New York, March 30, 1977. Earlier, Mrs. Neil Armstrong, wife of the first man on the moon, christened the sister ship *Cunard Countess* at San Juan, Puerto Rico, August 8, 1976.

gion, with high ratings from critics evaluating the opportunities for vacations in the Caribbean.

The June 27, 1977, sailing from Southampton coincided with the dress rehearsal for the Jubilee Review of the Fleet by Her Majesty the Queen. While the passengers and crew lined the decks, the loudspeakers on the *Queen* played "Land of Hope and Glory" and "Rule, Britannia," which provided many emotional moments for those watching the proceedings. There were 180 vessels in the review line and hundreds of pleasure craft all over the water. Two Royal Naval vessels, H.M.S. *Ark Royal* and H.M.S. *Huron*, at the end of the line, had to be pushed apart by tugs as they were swinging to the tide in order to allow the *Queen* to pass through a 700-foot space between them. The *Queen Elizabeth 2* exchanged salutes with vessels all the way down the line in a most majestic departure from Southampton.

For economic reasons, it was decided that the 1977 annual refitting would be carried out by the Bethlehem Steel Corporation of Bayonne, New Jersey. By having the refit in the United States the ship was able to start the winter cruise season earlier without having to cross the North Atlantic at a time of the year when not very popular. Work included the renewal of one of the turbines. The turbine, weighing 17 tons, had to be flown out in a Lockhead Hercules aircraft from the makers: John Brown Engineering of Scotland. The dockyard also constructed and fitted the two most luxurious rooms on the ship, known as the Queen Elizabeth and Queen Mary suites.

One more rescue can be listed to the credit of the *Queen Elizabeth 2*—during

America's only major contribution to the superstructure of the *QE2* was made in 1977 when the Queen Mary and Queen Elizabeth Suites were fitted forward of the 1972 penthouses during an annual refit at the Bethlehem Steel Shipyard, Bayonne, New Jersey.

daylight hours, for a change. On passage from Cherbourg to New York on August 16, 1977, a message was received at 1000 hours from the French trawler *Drakker* of Dieppe saying that they required assistance for an injured seaman, Claude Leleu. The *Queen* altered course and rendezvoused with the *Drakker*. A launch was sent away from the *QE2* to collect Leleu, who was safely on board by 1120 hours. He was admitted to the ship's hospital and treated for leg injuries from which he fully recovered.

The desire to produce variety in the *Queen*'s schedule resulted in a decision for the liner to make a Great Pacific and Oriental Cruise in 1978 rather than another cruise around the world. The history-making 39,057-mile cruise saw visits to Australia, New Zealand, and the Philippines during which the *Queen Elizabeth 2* visited thirty-one ports, including twelve that she had never been to before.

Captain T. D. Ridley, R.D., R.N.R., was in command when the *Queen Elizabeth 2* experienced one of the worst storms of her career to date during a North Atlantic crossing in September 1978. The liner encountered a storm front lying across the shipping lanes, which gave little choice for maneuvering. The winds built up to Force 12, and the waves were 50 feet high. Captain Ridley commented that it was one of the worst storms he had experienced in thirty-five years at sea. At one point a wall of water hit the liner broadside on the bow and crumpled the iron railing, and colossal waves occasionally nearly reached as high as the bridge. According to a Newsweek article of September 25, 1978, a woman had asked Captain Ridley if he had considered asking the Coast Guard for assistance during the worst of the storm. Ridley had replied, "Madame, first there was no need for help. And, secondly, if there had been a Coast Guard cutter in the area, the *Queen* would have had to help the Coast Guard."

The *Queen Elizabeth 2* reached her tenth birthday in 1979 and the 1979–1980 period was celebrated appropriately as a milestone in her career. The 1979 world cruise, with the theme "For once in your life, live!" went to twenty-four ports in fourteen countries. Especially historical was the inaugural call at Darien, the first time in recent history that a passenger liner from the Western world has ever docked in the People's Republic of China. During the call, the Joe Loss band played at a concert attended by more than 1,700 Chinese, again, the first showband ever to do so. Another inaugural visit was to the island of Tristian da Cunha in the South Atlantic. In honor of the ship's arrival, islanders produced the longest British Commonwealth stamp ever issued.

During her tenth anniversary year the *Queen* also was the subject of a National Geographic film about the great ocean liners, which had enormous coverage in the United States and Europe. The film, titled *The End of an Era*, resulted in a new awareness of a vanishing piece of maritime heritage and the fact that the *Queen Elizabeth 2* was the last great transatlantic liner. During her first decade in service the *Queen* had steamed over one and a half million miles and carried the British flag to sixty-three nations around the world.

The *Queen* has more than her share of heroes. On October 24, 1979, she was in the harbor of Las Palmas when an elderly passenger fell into the water. Four *QE2* crew members who saw the accident did not hesitate to jump to the rescue. They were Cruise Director Brian Price; cruise staff members Eric Mason and George Schofiled; and Deputy Chief Engineer Stanley Child. The four men dived between the ship and quayside in deep water, and although they dragged the passenger to shore, he died approximately a month later without leaving the hospital. Captain Douglas Ridley congratulated the men on their courage and Mr. Bernard Crisp, Cunard's marketing director, presented them with awards. Mr. Crisp said: "Some of us go through life never having the opportunity to find out if we are really brave. I believe anybody on this ship would have done what you did—but the difference is that you actually did it."

The 1979 refitting was undertaken by Bethlehem at Bayonne between November 21 and December 21, 1979, and resulted in extensive work on the boilers in cooperation with the British firm of Foster-Wheeler Ltd., which had designed and built the units originally. The complete overhaul of auxiliary equipment was undertaken as well as work on one propeller, the stabilizers, and some bilge plating. What is most important to passengers, of course, is what they see and, perhaps, how they see it. The 1979 refit saw the replacing of 25,000 fluorescent light bulbs to put a shine on the facelift, along with 20 miles of carpeting, and the repainting of her hull with self-polishing paint.

During the Tenth Anniversary World Cruise in 1980, one of the highlights of the trip was the maiden transit of the Suez Canal, making the *QE2* the largest ship ever to transit both the Suez and Panama canals in the same voyage. The inaugural call to Yalta on the shores of the Black Sea was unexpectedly short. As passengers were preparing to go ashore in the launches, the

One of the great cruises of the *Queen Elizabeth 2* nearly every year is the Canada and Atlantic Isles cruise. A frequent high point of this trip is the visit to Quebec, where the *Queen* now docks in the shadow of the Plains of Abraham and the Château Frontenac (August 1983).

Russian authorities decided that every shoregoing passenger must have a Soviet visa. The fact was brought to the attention of Captain R. H. Arnott, who realized right away that the process of carrying out the authorities' wishes would take so long that some of the passengers would never get ashore. Without further ado, he ordered all the officials off the ship and put to sea again as the stirring music of 'Rule, Britannia' played throughout the liner.

It was on a crystal-clear day in Geiranger Fjord on May 29, 1980, that the first known launching of a hot-air balloon was made from the deck of a British passenger ship. Mr. Ola Kalvatn brought his hot-air balloon on board the *QE2*, where it was inflated on the after end of One Deck, and with then-Chief Officer Ronald Warwick as crew lifted off. It made a twenty-five-minute flight across the fjord and landed in a field near the town of Geiranger.

The officers of the *Queen* were able to contribute something to the happy solving of an Atlantic mystery in June 1980. The two-masted schooner *El Pirata*, en route from Boston to Kristiansand, Norway, had not been seen or heard from since June 11 and was reported overdue by Portishead Radio. On June 22, the schooner was sighted 923 miles from Lands End. All was reported well except that problems had been experienced with their radio.

The 1981 world cruise of the *Queen Elizabeth 2* was named The Six Continent Odyssey and began from New York on January 18, 1981. The *Queen* sailed around the world on an eastward course through the Panama Canal and across the Pacific for a total distance of 32,946 miles in eighty days.

Upon returning from the world cruise, the *QE2* sailed into a sea of labor troubles at Southampton Docks. As a result she was unable to store much in the way of provisions and had to make arrangements to take on supplies at a number of cruise ports, notably Lisbon. In May 1981 she had to terminate a cruise at Cherbourg and to turn around there when dockers, who had refused to handle the passengers of the Peninsular and Orient (P & O) Steamship

The *Queen* slowly moves toward the new quay adjacent to the Old Town of Quebec, which was founded by the French and dates back to the early seventeenth century. The docking operation against the current of the mighty Saint Lawrence must be handled with care. (Photo courtesy of James MacLachlan.)

Company liner *Canberra*, also refused to serve the *Queen*. The 1981 transatlantic season began from Cherbourg as the result of Southampton labor unrest. On May 22, when the ship was preparing to sail, the crane drivers would not lift off the gangway. Captain Ridley instructed his sailors to cut it off with gas torches in order to permit the liner to sail on a Norwegian cruise.

A major modernization of the facilities at Southampton resulted in the closing of the old Southampton Ocean Terminal, which had served all three *Queens* and many other big ships for forty years. In its place the new Queen Elizabeth II Terminal was created for the handling of the passengers and luggage from the *Queen* and opened in April 1981.

Cunard designated the July 25–30, 1981, crossing from New York to Southampton the *QE2* Royal Wedding Commemorative Voyage. The ship was decorated in honor of the prince and princess of Wales, and special programs and lectures were given during the crossing. As a finale, a specially made film of the royal wedding in St. Paul's Cathedral was flown out to the *Queen* by helicopter for showing in the theater during the last day out. Passengers were delighted with the experience and expressed their appreciation to Cunard for not having missed the wedding of the century.

Every now and then the ship has to deal with a stowaway. Piccolo, a rather thin mongrel that lives in New York near the pier at West Forty-ninth Street, had become acquainted with one of the *QE2*'s sailors, who smuggled him aboard for a good meal. However, he was soon discovered in the crew quarters after the ship sailed. He was promptly confined to the kennels, which are located near the Penthouse Suites. There were no other dogs on board so he enjoyed the luxury of his own kennel maid and a choice of cuisine from the Queen's Grill kitchen. Unbeknown to those on the ship, the dog's owner was distressed about the loss of her pet and contacted Cunard to ensure that he

One of the most dramatic experiences a cruise or an Atlantic crossing can offer is a night sailing. These do not occur too often, but when they do the *Queen Elizabeth 2* is a dramatic sight as she slowly backs out into the North River, with all her lights ablaze and enough electricity being expended to supply a city of 20,000.

was returned. When the ship arrived in New York from the Bahamas cruise, Piccolo's mistress was there to meet him, accompanied by four television camera crews and several news reporters.

In 1982 the *Queen Elizabeth 2* was invited to Philadelphia for the celebrations in connection with the three hundredth anniversary of the city, "Century Four." The events in connection with this maiden voyage to Delaware Bay and what followed would make for one of the most exciting episodes in the life of the *Queen*.

CHAPTER SIX

The Falklands

The maiden arrival of the *Queen Elizabeth 2* in Philadelphia on April 25, 1982, was all that anyone could have desired. This special occasion was marked by the grand opening of "Century Four," the year-long tricentennial celebration (1682–1982) of the founding of the city of Philadelphia by William Penn. The reception given the *Queen* was exuberant even if security precautions were tight. After four days of celebrations, the *Queen Elizabeth 2* put out to sea again on April 29, for what everyone thought would be a normal passage to England.

All of the *Queen*'s officers were concerned about the outbreak of hostilities between Great Britain and Argentina over the Falkland Islands, some 8,000 miles away in the wintry South Atlantic, but few thought there was much likelihood of the *QE2* ever becoming involved. However, their thoughts proved to be wrong when the news was received, through unofficial channels, that she was to be requisitioned for trooping duties. On May 3, as the *Queen* steamed along the south coast of England bound for Southampton, those on board listening to the 1230 BBC news heard that their ship had been requisitioned by the government. Following confirmation, Captain Alexander J. Hutcheson made a formal announcement to passengers and crew that the *QE2* would be withdrawn from commercial service upon arrival at Southampton.

The conversion work began almost immediately after disembarkation and the landing of nearly 80 tons of baggage. With a few structural alterations, the large, broad, open expanses of the *Queen*'s decks, both fore and aft, were perfectly suited for helicopters. The Upper Deck Lido in line with

Preparing the *Queen Elizabeth 2* for her duties as a troop transporter/helicopter carrier included the construction of an after flight deck for helicopters on the stern of the ship.

Below the new flight deck it was necessary to strengthen the structure in order to provide firm landing platforms for the helicopters and their loads.

the Q4 Bar* as well as all the associated superstructure down to the Quarter Deck level was sliced off. This enabled the after end of the *QE2* to be converted into one huge landing pad and service area. The question of what would support the enormous weight of the steel pads and Sea King helicopters plus whatever else it might be called upon to carry was critical. The two outdoor swimming pools aft were the answer as they were designed to hold tons of seawater and therefore could supply the foundation for the flight deck. Steel plates were laid over the bottoms of the pools to support and distribute the weight of a network of vertical girders. Forward, the Quarter Deck toward the bow was extended over the capstan machinery in order to create a second landing pad.

Secure communications in any war situation are very important, so an independent radio room to house secret equipment was constructed behind the bridge. Because the *Queen* could not carry fuel for much more than a one-way trip, provisions had to be made for refueling at sea. Pipes were laid from the starboard midships baggage entrance on Two Deck down to the huge tanks of the liner six decks below.

Between May 5 and 9, most of the decorative pictures, valuable furniture, plants, and casino equipment were removed from the ship and stored in warehouses ashore. The *Queen*'s own china, glassware, and silverware was packed up and stored. In an effort to protect the carpeting, sheets of hardboard were laid over carpets in the public rooms, passageways, stairways, and in some of the cabins. Some of the deep blue carpet of the "D" Stairway was taken up and stored, exposing the bare deck, which could better withstand the wear and tear from soldiers' boots.

*Now the Yacht Club.

A view of the *QE2*, taken from a Sea King helicopter as it circles the huge liner in the South Atlantic and begins an approach to the stern landing area.

As the *Queen* received tons upon tons of military stores and equipment, the news was received that H.M.S. *Sheffield*, a British destroyer, had been hit by an Exocet missile fired from an Argentinean Super Etendard plane. There were heavy casualties, including twenty dead. The sinking of the *Sheffield* followed by two days the torpedoing of the second largest ship in the Argentinean navy, the *General Belgrano* (ex-U.S.S. *Phoenix*), which sank in the icy waters of the South Atlantic. The war clearly was heating up for both sides, with grievous losses in men and ships. Suddenly Cunard officers and crew who were being given sporadic leave began to be more concerned about writing wills and setting their personal affairs in order. In manning the ship for the voyage to the war zone, Cunard sought volunteers. Approximately 650 were chosen out of over 1,000 who had stepped forward.

The equipment being loaded on the *Queen* included hundreds of extra life jackets and additional safety appliances. The ammunition assigned to the ship for transport was stored in No. 1 hold, although additional quantities in containers were loaded on the Sports Deck forward of the funnel near what was normally the kennels. Other items loaded included land rovers, trailers, helicopter parts, fuel, and rations. The combination of high-octane aviation fuel and ammunition in containers on open decks with the possibility of an Exocet missile attack was hair-raising, but virtually no location on the *QE2* offered much security against such an event.

Finally, after eight whirlwind days of creating a fighting unit from the chaos of conversion, the *Queen Elizabeth 2* was ready to receive her most important military cargo. The embarkation of troops began at 0545 hours on May 12, with regimental bands on hand to pipe the men aboard. By 1430 hours, approximately 3,000 men of the Fifth Infantry Brigade, comprising units of the Scots Guards, the Welsh Guards, and the Gurkha Rifles, had embarked. At

Critical to the success of the *Queen Eliza-beth 2* as a troop transport and helicopter carrier was the ability to refuel the vessel. A practice refueling exercise with R.F.A. *Grey Rover* occurred along the south coast of England soon after the *Queen* began her voyage.

1603 hours, under the command of Captain Peter Jackson, the *Queen Eliza-beth 2* put to sea bound for the South Atlantic. The dockside was crowded with family members and well-wishers waving to the ship and to the sound of a Scottish bagpipe rendering "Scotland the Brave." As the *QE2* steamed slowly along the Solent, the aircraft landing pads received their first baptism as two Sea King helicopters touched down on the ship. Their rotors were folded back and they were speedily secured for the voyage.

The principal job for the afternoon of the first day at sea was to experiment with at-sea replenishment of the *Queen*'s fuel bunkers. She sailed from Southampton with 5,969 tons of fuel oil, but that was barely enough to get her to her destination in the South Atlantic. Somewhere and somehow, securing more fuel would be imperative. The *Queen* headed westerly to a rendezvous point in the Channel with the Royal Fleet Auxiliary tanker *Grey Rover*. As the *Grey Rover* approached from the stern on the starboard side, a lightweight rocket line was fired across to the *QE2*. This line was attached to a second, in-termediate line, which was attached to the "messenger." The two ships took up position about 150 feet apart and a distance line was run across from the two forecastles. About 100 soldiers heaved up the slack in the "messenger" and then pulled over an 8-inch flexible fuel line. The hose was connected to

One of the most important reasons for requisitioning the *QE2* was her ability to deliver physically fit troops and pilots to the war zone. Soldiers exercised in full kit so that their training and conditioning would make them fit for whatever challenges might materialize.

A portion of the ammunition carried by the *Queen* was intended for troop practice sessions. Firing exercises frequently took place from the Boat Deck, at small floating targets released from a forward shell door as they swept by the liner. Care had to be taken to restrain enthusiasm so that no bullets came too near the liner.

the *QE2*'s new bunker line, permitting the system to be tested by the passage of several tons of oil from the tanker to the *Queen*'s fuel tanks. With the success of the experiment, the line was drained of oil, disconnected, and paid back out to *Grey Rover* for retrieval. The *Queen Elizabeth 2* then proceeded south, avoiding the normal sea lanes on a 3,000-mile track toward Freetown, Sierra Leone.

Physical fitness was of paramount importance to the troops aboard the *QE2*. Every unit was given an assigned time period for jogging around the boat deck, starting at 0630 hours. The noise of hundreds of men in full kit and boots jogging was deafening.

Some of the ammunition on the ship was intended for firing practice, and this daily routine commenced on May 15. Every part of the ship was utilized for some form of training. Giant wall maps of the Falklands and the South Atlantic were spread across the bulkhead by the "G" staircase on the quarter-deck, where tapestries of the launching of the *Queen* previously had hung. A newfound interest in South Atlantic geography was noted on the part of passers-by. Another daily routine as the *Queen* steamed southward was flying practice for the crews of the Sea King helicopters. Several hours a day were devoted to this, in part because no one actually knew where they would be required to disembark the troops or in what manner the disembarkation might be accomplished.

After six days at sea, at 0900 hours on Tuesday, May 18, the Cape Sierra Leone lighthouse was sighted and the ship made her approach into Freetown Harbor. The stop at Freetown, to replenish fuel and water supplies, was a cal-

The most dramatic part of the training sessions as the *Queen Elizabeth 2* steamed southward was the Sea King helicopter take-off and landing exercises, which always drew an admiring crowd. The pilots found that the aft landing pads required some time for familiarization. The landing pad guidelines ultimately were extended to the sides of the ship in order to increase visibility.

culated risk, but it meant that the *Queen* could proceed to her final destination without danger of running low. Security was such that the *Queen Elizabeth 2* slipped in and out of Freetown unnoticed by the world's press.

One of the most critical tasks on the *Queen Elizabeth 2* after she left Freetown was the creation of a total ship blackout. There are an awful lot of portholes on the *QE2*, not to mention hundreds of large public-room windows. At the same time, in tackling the problem there was no desire to apply black paint everywhere if anything else would do. Black plastic, such as that used for garbage bags, came to the rescue for temporary service.

Ascension Island lay only a day and a half's steaming from Freetown. Shortly after her arrival on Friday, May 20, a further 200 tons of stores and bags of mail were transferred to the ship by helicopter. Later, Major General J. J. Moore, commander of land forces, and his command staff arrived on board, having flown out from the United Kingdom to Ascension to join the ship.

On Sunday, May 23, as the *Queen Elizabeth 2* headed southward on the last leg of her outward voyage, the radar was turned off and the ship was electronically silenced. Modern radar is a great boon to navigation, but in wartime a dead giveaway as to the location of a ship. From dawn to dusk military lookouts were posted on the bridge wings as well as near the funnel. The watertight doors on decks 6, 7, and 8 had been shut earlier, but as the ship steamed closer to the war zone all other watertight doors were closed as a safety precaution.

The closer the *QE2* got to the war zone, the keener the attention paid to the news. Before May 21 not too much happened, but after that, with the landing on San Carlos by the British on May 22, and with the news of the successful

Argentinean strikes against the Cunard Line container ship *Atlantic Conveyor* and the naval ships *Ardent*, *Antelope*, and *Coventry*, the war was suddenly a reality. To those listening on the *Queen*, the air raids against British ships seemed incessant, even if the Argentineans were taxing their men and planes to the limit. The loss of the captain and some of the crew of the *Atlantic Conveyor* was disturbing because some of them were known to those on the *QE2*. On May 24 the construction of platforms on the bridge wings was completed to hold the mounting for .5 Browning machine guns. The Browning machine guns could fire eight hundred rounds a minute. In addition, 7.62-millimeter general purpose machine guns and Blow Pipe Air Defense Missiles were located in strategic positions. These were the only armaments carried for the *Queen*'s own protection.

By May 26, the *Queen* was near enough to the active war zone that she began to zigzag rather than just steering variable courses as before. During the night of May 26–27, mist settled in around midnight, and visibility was reduced substantially and the presence of ice became ever more ominous. The situation in the darkness rapidly deteriorated to such a critical level that the danger from the numerous icebergs was considered far greater than that from hostile forces. Captain Jackson had gone to the bridge as the fog settled in. He consulted with the naval authorities as the *QE2* was forced to slow her speed and to weave between the giant bergs. Finally, in spite of the danger of revealing the ship's position, the radar was turned on. The possibility of the *Queen* becoming trapped by icebergs or colliding with one was a more imminent risk than discovery by the enemy. During the next six hours many icebergs of monstrous proportions suddenly loomed out of the misty darkness and at one time over 100 bergs large enough to be seen by the radar were on the scan. Each of those great masses of ice could sink a ship. The largest of the gigantic bergs was over a mile long — six times the length of the *Queen* — and at 300 feet high must have weighed in at several million tons. As dawn broke, the iceberg danger was past, although one huge berg could still be seen seven miles from the *Queen*, soaring above the low-lying mist and probably towering 200 to 300 feet above the rolling South Atlantic Ocean. It was so huge that it looked like the white cliffs of Dover while another seemed like cathedral spires rising from the sea. As the sun rose, the icebergs reflected a rainbow of colors in magnificent shades of red, orange, and yellow.

A rendezvous with H.M.S. *Antrim* was planned for noon on Thursday, May 27, in order to transfer Major General Moore and Brigadier Wilson with their advance headquarters. Before Brigadier Wilson left the *QE2*, he penned a parting message for publication in the "5th Infantry Brigade/*QE2* News" that summed up the role of the soldiers and the liner to that date:

> Very shortly we shall all transfer to other ships off South
> Georgia and start on the last phase of our move to the Falk-

The principal human settlement from the days of the whaling industry in South Georgia was Grytviken, although the site had been abandoned as a working community. The spark that started the war occurred when Argentinian workers, brought here to dismantle the whaling station for scrap, raised the Argentine flag and thereby produced a chain reaction that resulted in hostilities.

land Islands. It looks as if the Brigade will be there about 1st June, that is early next week. Once there, we shall join 3 Commando Brigade. We shall sort ourselves out; and then start joint operations to recapture the islands. Orders will be given out on landing. It is too early yet to issue a detailed plan, for it would be bound to change over the course of the next five days. This is the final issue of this newspaper, and to the Master and ship's company of *QE2*, I would say "Thank you" for the way you have looked after us on this voyage. We have come to know you well, we admire you, and we shall always be proud that we sailed with you in your magnificent ship. To the Brigade I would simply say this: "We shall start earning our pay as a team shortly; and we are in this game to win!

At 1804 hours on May 27, Right Whale Rocks, South Georgia, was four and one-half miles away but visibility was virtually nil; the short South Atlantic winter day had already given way to night and thick fog. By 1922 hours, just under nine days after leaving Southampton, the vessel was safely at anchor. The *Queen*'s anchorage was in Cumberland Bay East, approximately one mile from the old whaling station at Grytviken, the origin of the whole conflict.

Cumberland Bay was the meeting place for the *QE2* and the ships that took her troops and equipment on to the Falkland Islands some 200 miles to the west. Other ships at the rendezvous were the Peninsular and Orient (P & O) liner *Canberra*, the North Sea ferry *Norland*, H.M.S. *Endurance*, and H.M.S. *Leeds Castle*. Also on hand to lend assistance were five converted trawlers— *Cordella, Farnella, Junella, Northella,* and *Pict*—all requisitioned and fitted out to form the 11th Mine Countermeasures Squadron. Shortly before midnight, the first group of 700 troops started to transfer from the *Queen* to the *Canberra*

The morning sunlight brilliantly lights one of the snow-capped peaks of South Georgia as seen from the afterdeck of the *QE2* in Cumberland Bay. A few crew members stop to admire the breathtaking beauty of the landscape.

As dawn broke on May 28, those on the *QE2* had their first view of Cumberland Bay, South Georgia, with the *Canberra*, dubbed the "great White Whale" by her troops, at anchor nearby. The 45,000-ton P & O liner would see a great deal of service in the South Atlantic before her return to Britain.

and *Norland*. Despite the late hour the soldiers were in good spirits and seemed anxious to be on the move. Dawn the following morning brought the first real view of Cumberland Bay and the surrounding mountains. Snow-

A dusting of snow blanketed the flight decks of the *QE2* on her second day at Grytviken, South Georgia. Graffiti instantaneously appeared in the new-fallen snow on the flight decks of the *QE2*, as few could resist the impulse to be creative.

The *QE2* is shrouded in an icy fog in Cumberland Bay East, South Georgia, as trawlers work energetically to remove men and supplies from the liner. The photograph was taken from one of the *Queen's* launches while it transported a small party of Cunard personnel to see the whaling station at Grytviken.

capped peaks spawned glaciers that flowed to the sea, calving numerous small icebergs in the waters of the bay.

The transfer of the troops and stores continued at daybreak using the helicopters and trawlers, the admiralty tug *Typhoon*, and the *QE2*'s launches. By evening most of the troops had disembarked and the Sea King helicopters were permanently transferred to the *Canberra*.

Snow started to fall on May 29 and by daybreak it had settled everywhere. The snow was beautiful, but potentially treacherous to work in. Nevertheless, more than one hundred tons of cargo still had to go. This was loaded into trawlers for transfer to H.M.S. *Stromness*, which had arrived shortly before noon. Later in the afternoon, some 640 survivors of the sunken H.M.S. *Ardent*, H.M.S. *Coventry*, and H.M.S. *Antelope* had joined the *QE2*. Many of the survivors of the lost Royal Navy vessels had little more than the clothes on their backs, and some of those were ragged. The officers and crew of the *QE2*

The grave of the intrepid British Antarctic explorer, Sir Ernest Shackleton, lies in the wind-swept cemetery at Grytviken. Many naval visitors have paid their respects at the site and left their ship emblems in tribute.

did their best to make them feel welcome. Most of the survivors could be accommodated in normal cabins, but the hospital of the *Queen* was soon full of the more critical casualties, who were described by the medical staff as being lucky to be alive.

The barometer fell steadily throughout the day and the weather gave cause for concern. The swell coming in the entrance to Cumberland Bay East made it increasingly difficult for the trawlers to come alongside with safety. Meanwhile, a report was received that the tanker *British Wye* was under attack 400 miles due north. The incident was a particular cause for concern as the tanker was a considerable distance from the mainland and to the north of South Georgia. By deduction this meant that the *QE2* was in range of attack as long as she remained in the area. Later it was learned that the Argentineans had used a Boeing *707* with a substantial cruising range to survey the South Atlantic at 18,000 feet searching for the *Queen Elizabeth 2*. It was decided that the *Queen* should sail away from danger and at 1727 hours she put to sea with 60 tons of ammunition still remaining on board.

The fuel situation was becoming increasingly acute as night fell on May 31. A rendezvous was made with the R.F.A. tanker *Bayleaf*, but conditions on Monday and Tuesday were too severe for any attempt at fuel transfer and the arrangements had to be canceled. By Wednesday, June 2, the options were considerably reduced with the liner down to less than 1,000 tons of fuel. Speed was reduced to 10 knots and a course set to facilitate pipeline connecting. The *Bayleaf* came up on the *Queen*'s starboard side and shortly after 0900 hours the pipe was secured and pumping commenced. The two ships were rolling along 150 feet apart with the sea boiling between them. Their violent movements at times made the hose appear to be almost horizontal. All day the ships kept po-

After leaving South Georgia, the *Queen Elizabeth 2* encountered gale-force winds that made refueling operations with the fleet oiler *Bayleaf* treacherous. By June 2, the *Queen* was down to less than 1,000 tons of fuel (less than two days' supply at full speed), and it was imperative to attempt transferring the precious fuel from the tanker to the liner.

sition, with the tanker having the additional responsibility of keeping station on the *Queen Elizabeth 2* rather than the other way around, as is normal when refueling takes place between naval vessels. At 1835 hours, after twelve hours, the decision was made to cease refueling because the pipeline clearly was chaffing and night was descending fast. By that time the *Queen* had taken on board almost 3,834 tons of fuel, which would be sufficient to sustain operations at 25 knots.

Initially, it was thought that the survivors of the lost British ships would disembark at Ascension Island for the long flight home. However, on June 3, orders were received from the Ministry of Defence to return to Southampton. The *Queen Elizabeth 2* had succeeded so well in her assignment that she was no longer required in the war zone and could best serve the Crown by bringing the survivors home.

The *Queen* neared Ascension Island once again on June 4 and rendezvoused with H.M.S. *Dumbarton Castle* to transfer some seriously injured survivors and the 25 tons of ammunition that remained on board. By 1815 hours she had turned her bow northward, leaving the South Atlantic behind.

On June 6, Captain Jackson received a signal informing him that the liner would be returned to Cunard immediately upon her arrival in Southampton to be refitted for her peacetime role. The news also arrived and spread like wildfire through the ship that the *Queen Elizabeth 2* would be greeted in Southampton water by the Royal Yacht *Britannia* with Her Majesty Queen Elizabeth, the Queen Mother, on board to welcome them home.

The *Queen Elizabeth 2* entered the Solent via the Needles Channel at 0900 hours on June 11. Admiral Sir John Fieldhouse, commander in chief of the Royal Navy, and Lord Matthews arrived on board by helicopter to address the survivors and attend a press conference. As the *QE2* slowly steamed along the Solent the *Britannia* came into view with Her Majesty Queen Elizabeth,

The homecoming to Southampton on June 11 was spectacular, with welcoming escorts in the Solent. The survivors from the *Ardent, Antelope*, and *Coventry* lined the decks of the *Queen Elizabeth 2* to greet Her Majesty Queen Elizabeth, the Queen Mother, on the royal yacht.

Her Majesty Queen Elizabeth, the Queen Mother, stands on the aft deck of the *Britannia* to welcome the troops home.

the Queen Mother, waving to the ship from the afterdeck of the yacht. All those on the *Queen Elizabeth 2* gave three resounding cheers to Her Majesty. As the ships passed each other the Queen Mother sent a message to Captain Jackson that read:

> I am pleased to welcome you back as *QE2* returns to home waters after your tour of duty in the South Atlantic. The exploits of your own ship's company and the deeds of valor of those who served in *Antelope, Coventry*, and *Ardent* have been acclaimed throughout the land and I am proud to add my personal tribute.

Captain Jackson replied with the words:

> Please convey to Her Majesty Queen Elizabeth our thanks for her kind message. Cunard's *Queen Elizabeth 2* is proud to have been of service to Her Majesty's forces.

The two messages, engraved in silver, have been immortalized on a large plaque that can be seen on the Heritage Trail (see Chapter Nine).

As the *QE2* passed the Fawley oil refinery, every vessel, great and small,

Following the return to Southampton on June 11, 1982, the *QE2* was returned to the Cunard Line. The restoration of the ship as a five-star passenger liner took place at Southampton in the huge dock originally built to accommodate the *Queen Mary* and the *Queen Elizabeth*. The ship is shown in dry dock during the reconditioning.

The removal of the aft helicopter landing pads from the liner is underway in this dry dock photo. Although reconstruction to prepare for the Falklands was accomplished in less than a week (May 5 to May 12, 1982), reconditioning consumed the better part of nine weeks (June 12 to August 7, 1982).

whistled or shrieked a salute to the liner, filling the air with sounds normally reserved for a maiden voyage. Southampton Harbor was alive with small boats out to view the historic occasion of yet a third *Queen* returning from a war. A short time later, the ship was alongside and the gangway down. The naval survivors walked ashore over a red carpet, to be given a red rose and directed to a quiet area inside the terminal building for a private reunion with their families. The *QE2*'s crew disembarked via the forward gangway where hundreds of happy family members had gathered to greet them. It was an emotional day for everyone. The *Queen Elizabeth 2* was home safe and sound, having completed a mission that took her 14,967 miles in just under thirty days.

CHAPTER SEVEN

The New *QE2*

On August 7, 1982, the *Queen Elizabeth 2* put to sea for twenty hours of engine trials following her refitting after service in the South Atlantic. It had taken only seven days to convert the *QE2* into a troopship, but to restore her took the better part of nine weeks. Following the removal of the two helicopter pads, a considerable amount of structural restoration had to be carried out, as well as internal refurbishing.

The time that the government required to restore the ship gave Cunard a unique opportunity to make several improvements of their own. Among the new facilities installed was the Golden Door Spa at Sea. This proved to be popular with health- and weight-conscious travelers of all ages, and the idea was ultimately extended to other Cunard ships. The Queen's Grill was redesigned and the casino expanded and redecorated. The first stage of the new Club Lido was carried out, which involved the repositioning of the bar and the fitting of glass doors at the after end leading out onto the open deck. The results were striking and received many favorable comments.

Certainly the most noticeable change was in the color scheme of the liner. The dark gray hull was repainted with a light gray that was almost white, and the funnel was painted in the traditional Cunard red with the two black bands. The goal was to give the *QE2* a new appearance after her return from trooping duties. However, the gray hull was very difficult to maintain in pristine condition and some paint was always lost when using tugs or from dockside fenders. After a reasonable trial period, it was decided to revert to the original dark gray. She was repainted in June 1983.

The "Pride of the British Merchant Fleet" sailed from Southampton on Au-

The reconditioning of the *QE2* following her return from the Falklands is nearly completed. The most striking aspect of this was the repainting of the hull to pebble gray as part of her new image. Astern of the 67,703-ton *QE2* lies the 44,807-ton *Canberra*, the second largest passenger liner in the British Merchant Marine, which also was being reconditioned after service in the South Atlantic.

Pristine in her new color scheme, the *Queen Elizabeth 2* returned to service in August 1982. In June 1983, the decision was made to return to a darker, gray hull that was substantially easier to maintain.

gust 15, 1982, with a full complement of passengers destined for New York. Thousands of well-wishers gave her a rousing send-off. Wessex helicopters flew overhead in salute, and a flotilla of small boats accompanied her out into the Channel. Prior to her departure Cunard chairman Lord Matthews hosted a reception on board. In his speech he stated that Cunard was delighted to have the *Queen Elizabeth 2* back in service. The *Queen*, he said, was unique and, giving existing commercial conditions, was likely to remain so for the rest of her life. She was the last of the great transatlantic ocean liners.

At the end of the 1982 season, Her Royal Highness Queen Elizabeth, the Queen Mother, paid a personal tribute to the liner when she visited the ship at Southampton on December 2. The Queen Mother toured the ship with Lord Matthews and Captain Peter Jackson and spoke to many members of the

The first arrival of the *QE2* to New York in August 1982 virtually qualified as a second maiden arrival as New Yorkers celebrated the return of the largest ship to use the North River passenger ship terminal on a regular basis. The scene when she sailed was a little quieter. The *Queen* passes the twin towers of the World Trade Center, which, at 1,250 feet, are only 25 percent taller than she is long.

ship's company who had sailed to South Georgia. She presented a handsomely embossed silver plaque to the ship to commemorate the vessel's service in the Falkland Campaign. The plaque records the messages exchanged between the Queen Mother and Captain Jackson while the *QE2* was steaming past the royal yacht in the Solent on her return voyage. The plaque is now on display between the Casino and the Golden Lion Pub on the Upper Deck.

In January 1983 the *Queen Elizabeth 2* set forth on her annual long cruise, now named The Great Pacific and Oriental Odyssey. The liner sailed from New York to Florida and the Caribbean and then via the Panama Canal to the west coast of Mexico and as far north as San Francisco before heading south toward the Tahitian Islands in the South Pacific and on toward New Zealand and Australia. Following a maiden call at Brisbane, the *QE2* turned northward through the Great Barrier Reef to Indonesia and the Orient. The visit to China and Japan remained one of the key attractions of the cruise. The *Queen* is regarded as a great tourist attraction in Japan, and thousands of people visit the docks to see her when she is in port. The homeward leg of the cruise across

St.VINCENT $2

Visit of the "QUEEN ELIZABETH 2" to KINGSTOWN, St.VINCENT

GORDON DRUMMOND   1982   FORMAT

Over the life of the *QE2* several countries have issued postage stamps featuring the ship. This stamp shows the hull painted pebble gray, and the funnel painted the traditional Cunard colors. The new livery appeared in 1982, after she returned from the Falkland Campaign.

the North Pacific is one of the single longest stretches of the cruise, but the great speed of the *Queen* turns it into a pleasurable break before the call at the Hawaiian Islands and the return to California. A west-to-east Panama Canal cruise brought the second transit of the waterway for the year and placed the *Queen Elizabeth 2* in New York for the beginning of the 1983 transatlantic season.

In May 1983, Trafalgar House and the Cunard Line announced the completion of successful negotiations to purchase the fleet and good will of

San Francisco is one of the most magnificent natural harbors in the world. The passage under the Golden Gate Bridge heralds the arrival of the *Queen* in one of the most cosmopolitan cities in the world.

The ms *Sagafjord* was launched in 1964 and purchased by Cunard Line in 1983. This highly rated cruise ship was an important addition to the fleet when the company began to expand into the luxury market. She was sold in 1997, and the new owners renamed her *Sagarose*.

The ms *Vistafjord* was launched in 1972 and purchased by Cunard Line at the same time as the ms *Sagafjord* in 1983. She is considered one of the most luxurious ships afloat and will be renamed *Caronia* in late 1999.

The slate-gray hull scheme was restored in June 1983, but the traditional Cunard funnel was retained. The *Queen* is shown as she was from late June 1983 to late December 1983, when the Lido Deck was reconstructed at Bremerhaven.

Norwegian American Cruises for $73 million. The two prizes gained were the magnificent passenger liners *Sagafjord* and *Vistafjord*. By this acquisition, Cunard was able to avoid the high costs of new construction and at the same time increase their fleet with two ships that consistently received the "five-star-plus" rating given by the Fieldings Guide to Cruising.

Also in May 1983, Trafalgar House announced that they had acquired a 5 percent holding in the Peninsular and Orient Steamship Company. P & O operates a large fleet of passenger liners and other vessels and is the only other major British line engaged in the passenger business. The subsequent takeover bid received a lot of publicity and was eventually referred to the Monopolies Commission in Great Britain for evaluation. The commission decided in the spring of 1984 that it would not be against the public interest for the bid to proceed. However, on September 11, 1984, Trafalgar House announced that it was selling its shares in P & O.

In the summer of 1983, the *Queen Elizabeth 2* set course for Skarsvag, Norway. When the ship anchored in the evening passengers were able to go ashore by tender and then take a forty-minute bus ride to the summit of the North Cape Plateau. Here, sheer cliffs rise over 1,000 feet above the Arctic Ocean. From this point one can watch the sun, at the midnight hour, nearly touch the horizon and slowly begin to rise. The entire face of the sun can be seen twenty-four hours a day from mid-May until the end of July. Norway's most dramatic monuments are the fjords. Geiranger Fjord, where the cliffs tower above the ship and the famous Seven Sisters Waterfalls can be seen cascading into the sea, is the most favored of all. While the *QE2* was at anchor in

The *QE2* rarely remains the same for a long period of time. A recent major improvement involved the covering of the Lido Deck pool with a retractable Magrodome, making it into an all-weather facility and vastly expanding the amenities of the ship. The work was done at Bremerhaven, Germany, and involved both extensive preparations and precision handling.

The aft end of the Club Lido (ex-Q4 Room) was sliced away on the North Atlantic by workmen who had joined the ship for the voyage. Then the Lido Deck was prepared for the Magrodome.

Geiranger on July 16, 1983, an old naval tradition took place on the bridge. At a ceremony attended by Captain Arnott and Chief Officer Warwick, the ship's bell was used as a font to christen six-week-old Cybelle Lisbeth Kalvatn.

Each fall the world's premier marathon race takes place in New York City. The race was set for October 23, 1983, and it attracted some 17,000 runners from all fifty states and sixty-eight foreign countries to compete in the event. Among the vast throng of runners at the start of the marathon were five members of the *QE2*'s crew, who had been training on board and at various ports around the world whenever the opportunity arose. The *Queen* was scheduled to dock in New York the morning of the marathon, but in order to be at the start on time, Cunard made arrangements for the runners to be picked up as the ship passed under the Verrazano Narrows Bridge. A launch came alongside the *QE2* to collect the runners and took them to Staten Island, where, after a quick BBC interview, the five were rushed by limousine to the assembly point for the start of the race. Many of the *Queen*'s crew members sponsored the New York Marathon runners, and as a result £1,778 ($2,700) was collected and shared by the National Lifeboat Institution and the Guide Dogs for the Blind Association. A guide dog was named Marathon, and his picture can be seen in one of the showcases on board the liner.

On November 28, 1983, the *Queen Elizabeth 2* arrived at Bremerhaven, Ger-

After the *Queen Elizabeth 2*'s return to the yard, the huge Magrodome was lifted from the yard by a powerful crane and positioned over the Lido Deck.

Once the positioning appeared exact, the Magrodome could be lowered onto the liner and welded in place. What had been one of the *Queen*'s two outside pools and rarely usable on the North Atlantic was transformed into a universal asset.

many, for her annual refitting. The announcement that the work, costing some £2 ½ million ($3,750,000), was being carried out in Germany generated adverse reaction in the British press. Very little attention was given to the fact that the major British shipyards had admitted they could not carry out the work on time, nor was much focus put on the fact that Cunard already had spent £11 million on the ship in British yards since June 1982. A huge passenger liner cannot lie idle and wait for a berth to come along. She must receive the needed services promptly and be back on the line earning revenue as quickly as possible. At Bremerhaven, the Magrodome,* a sliding glass roof, was fitted over the Quarter Deck swimming pool, making it available for use in all weather. Powerful new launches were added to assist in the transfer of passengers from ship to shore at anchorage ports. Various sections of the ship were redecorated and refurbished in line with Cunard's ongoing program to maintain the *QE2* as a vessel second to none.

By April 1984, the *Queen Elizabeth 2* had visited 145 different places around the world during the first fifteen years of her career. The most frequently visited port was New York, with 325 calls; Southampton, the *Queen* home port, was second, with 240 dockings.

The world belongs to the *QE2*, as much as the *Queen* to the world, since she is and remains unique. The 1984 great cruise was called The Quintessential

*Replaced by the Lido Restaurant in 1994.

At Bremerhaven, the hull was thoroughly cleaned and painted as part of the annual refit. The anchor chains are paid out so that each anchor and all the links may be checked and painted. Note the bulbous bow that reduces water friction and the bow thruster doors on each side of the hull, open for inspection.

The *Queen*'s original propeller dwarfs the workmen in the dry dock. Each of the six-bladed propellers weighed 31.75 tons and had a diameter of 19 feet. The propellers were replaced in 1987 by variable-pitch units with five blades each.

World Cruise. One of the highlights of this cruise occurred on February 29 at Port Kelang in Malaysia. At the invitation of His Royal Highness, the Sultan Salahuddin Abdul Aziz Shah of Selengor, and Her Royal Highness, the Tengku Ampuvan of Selengor, a banquet and entertainment in observance of the annual *Queen Elizabeth 2* World Cruise Society was held for over 300 passengers at the royal palace. A fitting indication of the importance of the *Queen* to other nations and their people was given in the message of His Royal Highness:

> I am privileged and honored to be given the opportunity to host this special function for the distinguished members of the World Cruise Society. Whilst it brings singular honors to me,

it is equally an honor for all Malaysians and the State of Selengor in particular.

On behalf of the people of Malaysia and the State of Selengor, I wish you all a very warm welcome and hope your stay here will be a pleasant and memorable one. We sincerely hope that this magnificent ship will call at Port Kelang on all its round-the-world trips, so that many more people can enjoy our warmth and hospitality, and, that whilst this beautiful vessel makes our world smaller, we can in our journeys mutually help to bring peace, understanding and happiness.

An Easter egg hunt was the special event arranged for children when the ship arrived at New York on April 22, 1984. But when a five-year-old girl found a silver Easter egg worth a free cruise on the *QE2*, she was heard to say that what she really wanted was a chocolate one!

The *QE2* is like a city at sea, but when that city reaches port it must rely on a considerable amount of support for its survival. Occasionally the shore operations department is taxed to the full extent to make arrangements that would normally be routine. Such was the case when the *QE2* was scheduled to arrive at Southampton on July 13, 1984, after a cruise with over 1,800 passengers on board. A sudden strike by dock workers in her home port of Southampton meant terminating the voyage across the channel at Cherbourg. This forced change in itinerary created a logistical challenge for the Cunard Line staff ashore as well as those on board. The purser's office was inundated with inquiries. Air transportation had to be chartered to take passengers and their baggage to England. Similar arrangements had to be made for those joining the ship for the transatlantic voyage to New York. It was a mammoth undertaking trying to contact all the passengers and crew, plus some dogs, cats, and cars, joining the ship, many of whom were already heading for the scheduled departure port of Southampton. The store managers both ashore and afloat had their own problems to deal with as provisions and technical equipment for the following voyage had to be air-freighted across the Channel. Yet despite all the difficulties, the *QE2* still managed to sail on time, main-

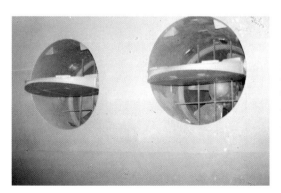

Bow thrusters enhance the *Queen*'s maneuverability. With the doors open, two variable-pitch propellers can be seen in through-hull tunnels. Each is 6.55 feet in diameter. When not in use, the doors fit flush against the hull.

The impressive size of the *Queen* is apparent as she passes a small yacht on an outward bound voyage from Southampton. (Photo courtesy of Alan Chandler.)

taining her schedule. Unfortunately, for a ship the size of the *Queen* these operations do not come cheaply, and the company had to face excess bills of hundreds of thousands of pounds.

To provide the ultimate combination of travel, the *Concorde* is extensively used by the Cunard Line to carry passengers to and from the *QE2* and their other cruise ships. On February 13, 1985, one of the supersonic aircraft was chartered to take passengers from London to Sydney, Australia, to join the world cruises of the *QE2* and *Sagafjord*—both in port together. The *Concorde* made the record-breaking trip in seventeen hours, three minutes, and forty-five seconds, including refueling stops at Bahrain, Colombo, and Perth. The following evening the *Queen Elizabeth 2* hosted a St. Valentine's Day ball, to which the passengers of the *Sagafjord* were invited.

The *Concorde* made her first commercial flight to South Africa the same year when she flew in to Cape Town with ninety-eight passengers who were joining the ship for the voyage to South America.

While off the coast of South Africa on March 25, 1985, the South African Air Force came to the assistance of the ship when they evacuated a sick crew member by helicopter and flew him to a hospital in Durban, where he later made a full recovery.

During the world cruise, the traditional Country Fair was held, and over

£16,100 ($21,500) was raised by passengers and crew. The selected charity for 1985 was the Jubilee Sailing Trust Fund. The charity was dedicated to building a sail training ship for the handicapped named the *Lord Nelson*. The three-masted barque is 150 feet long and it was designed and built to carry a crew of twenty physically handicapped and twenty able-bodied passengers. It is often seen sailing around the coast of England and the Continent.

Most maritime cities regard the first visit of a ship to the port as an important occasion, and events are arranged to make the arrival a special one. Such was the case when the *QE2* made her inaugural visit to Baltimore on May 5, 1985. With a flotilla approaching 2,000 boats as well as helicopters and planes circling overhead, the ship passed under the Chesapeake Bay Bridge and made a stately entrance into the port. The city of Baltimore gave a regal welcome to the ship and presented the passengers and crew with 5,000 long-stemmed red roses.

Three marvels of British technology came together in the English Channel on May 18, 1985, when the *QE2*, *Red Arrows*, and the *Concorde* were all photographed at the same time from a Hawk jet aircraft. It took months of careful planning to take this historic picture, as the ship and airplanes had to rendezvous in daylight hours in good weather and conditions.

On May 27, 1985, Captain T. D. Ridley was appointed commodore of the Cunard Line. He was the first master to be appointed to this rank since Commodore W. E. Warwick retired from the sea in 1972.

Like any city, a ship the size of the *QE2* cannot be without the occasional mystery. A British vacationer was reported missing by his wife when he did not return to his cabin by 2000 hours on 29 October 1985. Captain Lawrence Portet ordered a thorough search of the ship and when convinced that the man was not on board, the ship was turned around and the course retraced. Although searchlights were used in the approaching darkness, the search was abandoned when the captain considered that there was no chance of ever finding anyone in the choppy sea.

History was made during the 1986 world cruise when the first-ever TV transmissions were received at sea. Programs received included *NBC Nightly News* with Tom Brokaw and even the U.S. Super Bowl—the highlight of the American football season. The television signal was received from the Comsat satellite network on a gyroscopic antenna. The 1,100-pound antenna, over seven feet in diameter, was lowered in place by helicopter while the ship was in New York on January 14, 1986.

Another milestone in the life of the *QE2* was recorded while the ship was bound for New York on June 5, 1986. Mrs. Kim Holtvoigt gave birth to a baby, who was delivered by the ship's medical officer, Dr. Mike Beeney. She was named Lauren and took United States citizenship, after her parents.

The *Queen Elizabeth 2* participated in the Statue of Liberty centennial celebrations in New York Harbor on July 4, 1986. Cunard commissioned Garrards, the Crown jewelers of London, to make a "freedom torch" as a gift to the American people. The torch, four feet high, made of copper, and decorated with gilt, is a contemporary copy of the torch held by Miss Liberty. The gift left England on June 26, sailing from Southampton, and was presented to the National Maritime Historical Society in New York. It was escorted to the United States by a Polish immigrant family of four, Ryszard and Magdalena Olesiak and their two sons, Karol (age 7) and Jakub (age 3). Like many immigrants, this family viewed America for the first time from the decks of a ship—but theirs was the *Queen Elizabeth 2*. As the *QE2* sailed under the Verrazano Narrows Bridge, escorted by an armada of thousands of boats, a 100-foot American flag was unfurled over the side of the ship. Red, white, and blue balloons were released into the sky while red, white, and blue carnations were tossed into the river, saluting America as the ship passed the Statue of Liberty. With the traditional fireboat welcome she then anchored off Liberty Island, joining many other naval and commercial ships from several other countries also there for the celebrations. It is estimated that Cunard has carried over two million immigrants to the United States since the company was founded in 1839.

In August 1986, the Cunard Line added two more ships to the fleet by taking over the operation of the *Sea Goddess I* and *Sea Goddess II* from Norske Cruises. The two yacht-style cruise ships entered service in 1984 and 1985. They were built by Watsila in Finland, and each has fifty-eight staterooms for 116 passengers, with a crew complement of 89. The two ships are built like private yachts and designed to provide an all-inclusive voyage in a private and luxurious atmosphere. Their itineraries are worldwide and they often call at remote and exotic ports inaccessible to larger ships.

When the *Queen Elizabeth 2* sailed from New York on October 20, 1986, with Captain Portet in command and John Chillingworth as chief engineer, another milestone was reached in the history of the Cunard Line. This was the last transatlantic crossing before her steam-turbine propulsion plant was replaced with diesel engines. Thus ended 146 years of continuous steam service, which began with the paddle steamer *Britannia*, the first ship to establish a scheduled transatlantic service. By the time the *QE2* arrived at the dockyard in Bremerhaven, she had steamed 2,622,858 nautical miles since December 23, 1968, which represents over 120 times around the world.

CHAPTER EIGHT

The End of Steam

Several well-known engine designers and shipyards from around the world were invited by the Cunard Line in July 1983 to tender for the re-engining of the *QE2*. The decision to re-engine was made due to rising fuel costs, high maintenance and repair expenses, and the risk of engine failure in service. Extensive research by Cunard had revealed that replacing the steam turbines with a completely new engine plant would result in a reduction in engine room manning and a savings in fuel consumption in the region of 200 tons per day. While the designers had the freedom to propose the type of plant and the general arrangement of it, there were some strict criteria. The successful bidder would have to demonstrate that noise and vibration levels would not be higher than with the steam turbines, simultaneously carry out the upgrade of passenger and crew facilities, and complete the conversion work in less than six months against penalty clauses for late delivery. By the summer of 1985 the Cunard Line had decided that MAN-B&W diesel engines would be used. Soon thereafter, on October 24, 1985, a contract was signed with Lloyd Werft Shipyard in Bremerhaven to carry out what would be the biggest marine engineering conversion job in merchant shipping history. No United Kingdom shipyard submitted a tender to carry out the work; however, approximately 30 percent of the contract price was spent in the U.K. on various parts of the propulsion plant. Despite requests to the British government for financial assistance, they refused to contribute to the project. The contract, valued at £180 million, included the removal of the existing turbine plant, installation of new diesel engines, conversion of public rooms, improvements in the

One of the nine new diesel engines lies in the manufacturers' workshop. Each engine was assembled and tested ashore before being lifted into the ship through the access made by the removal of the funnel. (All photos on these two pages courtesy of Martin Harrison.)

Before the new engines could be fitted at Bremerhaven in 1986, 4,700 tons of metal had to be removed. Here a section of the original 250-foot propeller shaft has been cut and drawn out of the stern tube.

kitchens, refurbishment of passenger cabins, upgrade of crew accommodations and overhaul of the lifeboats and davits.

The *QE2* arrived at Bremerhaven on October 27, 1986, and soon after stripping out of the old propulsion plant began. The first major item to be removed was the funnel, to provide access down through the center of the ship to the engine room. Most of the old machinery was lifted out through the casing, and the new engines were lowered down the same way. Over 4,700 tons of metal was removed from the ship within the first five weeks.

After an estimated 1.7 million man-hours of work, the ship was delivered back to the owners 179 days later, on April 25, 1987.

Fitted with her new engines of 118,010 horsepower, the *Queen Elizabeth 2* became the world's most powerful marine propulsion plant. During the trial

One of the steam turbines that helped to propel the *Queen* over two million nautical miles lies on the dockside at Bremerhaven, destined for scrap.

The final section of the new 230-foot long port propeller shaft is being lined up to be inserted into the stern tube (at left). The outer end of the shaft is covered to protect the mechanism of the variable-pitch propeller blades.

she reached a speed in excess of 33 knots and demonstrated an emergency stop in three minutes and eighteen seconds in a distance of 1.1 miles.

To achieve this performance, the *Queen Elizabeth 2* is fitted with nine medium-speed diesel engines. Each engine weighs 220 tons and has an output of 10,620kW (14,242 hp) at 400 revolutions per minute. They are arranged athwartships in two groups: four in the forward engine room and five in the after engine room. The engines are secured in position on antivibration mountings.

Each diesel engine is connected with a flexible coupling to an alternator to produce electricity. Any axial movement of the rotor caused by the rolling and pitching of the ship in rough weather is overcome by thrust pads fitted to the front end bearings. A brushless excitation system provides the field for the eighteen pole generators using a permanent magnet exciter. The power from

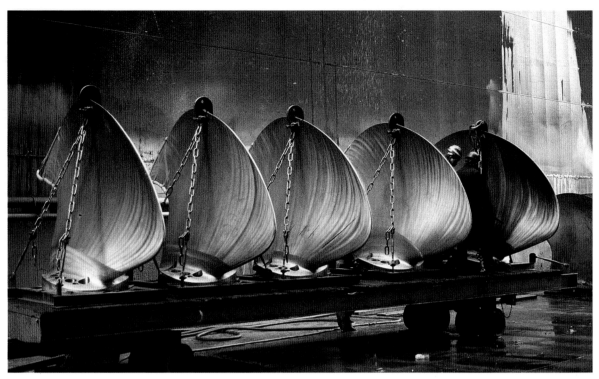

New highly polished variable-pitch propeller blades on the dock ready to be fitted to the shaft. Controls situated on the bridge can vary the angle of the blades, which enables the ship to be maneuvered in either direction without the need for a gear box or by reversing the engine. (Photo courtesy of Martin Harrison.)

all nine generators is fed directly to a common 10kV busbar system divided into two separate main switchboards. Each switchboard is installed in a separate compartment. The common busbar supplies the electricity to the two main propulsion motors. For domestic and ship's services use, the voltage is transformed to 3,300 volts for distribution throughout the ship. Further voltage reduction to 415v, 220v, and 110v is performed by transformers local to the sub-switchboards for various uses.

The propulsion motors, made by GEC Large Machines, Ltd., England, are believed to be the largest single-unit propulsion motors in commercial service. Each weighs 295 tons and is rated at 44MW synchronous running at 144 revolutions per minute. The motors have a diameter of about 30 feet, and, due to space constraints, they were made especially for the ship. A variable-frequency synchro convertor starting system makes it possible to start the motors without the high current that would be required directly from the generators. To allow for the ship to operate at maximum efficiency at slow speed, the constant propeller speed can be reduced to 72 rpm with the use of the 11MW convertors. Each motor is connected to a 230-foot-long propeller shaft inclined downward at 1.5 degrees to the horizontal extending sternward to each side of the rudder.

This picture shows the seven-bladed Grimm Wheels, which rotated freely on the propeller shaft and were designed to improve efficiency by recovering energy lost in the slip stream. Unfortunately some of the blades broke off during trials so the wheels were removed entirely and have never been replaced.

The two controllable pitch propellers, 22 feet in diameter, were made by Lips BV., Holland. They have five blades shaped to provide maximum thrust and at the same time reduce tip vortexes and cavitation. The design, to absorb 44MW at 144 rpm, makes them the most powerful CP propellers in the world. The pitch of the blades can be controlled from the engine control room or from the bridge.

The propellers were designed to function with Grimm Wheels. The seven-bladed vane wheels were fitted behind the propellers and freely rotate on the same shaft. These wheels are in use on other ships to reclaim part of the energy normally lost in the slip stream of the propeller and convert it into additional thrust. They were predicted to do the same on the *Queen Elizabeth 2* and to save 2 to 4 percent in fuel costs. Unfortunately, some of the vanes were lost during trials, so the remainder of the blades on both shafts were removed and not replaced.

The operation of the engine plant is fully automated by electronically controlled governors that help to ensure optimum efficiency and safety. In port, one diesel will remain on line for domestic services with another on standby, which will activate automatically should the need arise. When the ship is preparing to sail, the operator selects "ready to sail" mode, which causes three

Data from the engines and ancillary services is fed electronically to the Engine Control Room, which enables the officers on duty to monitor all aspects of the machinery. Closed-circuit television provides a constant visual surveillance of the machinery in twenty-six locations. (Photo courtesy of Robin Ebers.)

more diesel engines to come on line and a further two diesel units to come on standby. Lubricating oil pumps and ventilators are automatically started.

When all the conditions have been satisfied, the computer will indicate the "ready to sail" condition and maneuvering can commence. The next stage is "combinator" mode. This starts the two propulsion motors running at a speed of 72 rpm. At this time the propeller pitch is at zero. The power now available is about 11MW per shaft for ahead and 8MW per shaft for going astern. This will give a speed of about 15 knots ahead.

After the ship has left the harbor, "free sailing" mode is selected. This will cause the speed of the propulsion motors to be increased to 144 revolutions per minute and automatically synchronized on to the main busbar. The propeller pitch commensurate with the desired speed is selected by the telegraph unit, and additional diesel engines will automatically be activated as required to achieve the required power.

The Engine Control Room (ECR) was redesigned during the refitting to permit the machinery space to be left unmanned. With the aid of computerization, data are centrally collected in this one room. About 4,000 pieces of data, such as oil pressures, water and oil temperatures, voltages, and currents can be requested and displayed on screens. Critical values are highlighted. Closed-circuit television cameras monitor the machinery space in 26 locations. A panel is centrally located to indicate the rudder and propeller pitch angles, the speed and engine revolutions. Nearby are the levers to control the propulsion and associated machinery. These controls are duplicated on the bridge so that the ship can be operated from either position.

As far as possible, machinery is divided between the forward and after engine rooms, either of which can be operated independently to run the ship in the event of serious damage in the other. Emergency shutdown systems operated from the ECR include electrical switching to stop all pumps passing flammable liquid, ventilation fans, dampers, main engines, and boilers. A

The turbo-charger casings in the center of the picture are situated above the couplings connecting the engines to the alternators. Exhaust gas from each engine is carried to the funnel by the large trunkings on the left. Within the funnel, heat from the exhaust is recovered in specially designed boilers to provide steam to heat the fuel and domestic water. (Photo courtesy of Martin Harrison.)

Halon gas system is fitted for use in an emergency. In the event of fire the gas can be discharged from the storage cylinders in about twenty seconds after shutting down the machinery and sealing the compartment. This gas breaks the chain reaction in the combustion process and thus extinguishes the fire.

As part of the re-engining, the whole of the inside of the funnel had to be replaced. It was removed to carry out this work. Exhaust gas pipes and silencers for the nine diesel engines and space ventilation ducting were all fitted into a metal framework prefabricated ashore in two parts and then assembled on the ship. The original funnel casing, considerably widened, was then replaced over the new stack.

Twenty-four exhaust and supply ventilators have been fitted for ventilation to the engine rooms for supply of combustion air and heat removal. The ventilators can supply 2 million cubic meters per hour and remove 1.4 million cubic meters per hour.

For domestic power and services, any combination of the nine alternators can be operated to supply power to the common busbar. Via transformers, some of this power can be directed to the domestic busbar (up to 3,300 volts) to operate the heating, lighting, fans, and other auxiliary machinery throughout the ship.

Steam is still used for domestic heating and for heating water and fuel. When the ship is at sea the steam is provided by exhaust-gas boilers fitted to each of the diesel engine uptakes. Two auxiliary oil-fired boilers with a capacity of 25 tons per hour provide a back-up supply. An estimated 74 percent of all waste heat will be recovered. The new boiler plant was manufactured by Sunrod International AB of Sweden.

Fresh water is made by four SERCK vacuum evaporators having a total daily output of 1,000 tons per day. Heating for the evaporators is mainly provided by cooling water from the diesel engines. It can also be provided by steam-heated booster heaters so output can be maintained if the ship is on re-

The liner enters dry dock every two to three years for survey work, repairs, and maintenance to be carried out on the hull. To keep the number of days that the liner is out of service to a minimum, work continues throughout the day and night.

duced speed or if all the diesel engines are not running. In addition, there is a reverse osmosis plant that can produce up to 450 tons of fresh water a day.

The bilge and ballast pumping systems were completely renewed in the conversion areas and some tank modification and repairs were carried out. Pumping operations are activated from the Safety Control Room on Two Deck.

The two bow thruster units, one of which is twelve feet to the rear of the other, were supplied by Stone Manganese Marine, Ltd., London. Both are contained in separate tunnels that pass laterally through the hull about 18 feet below the water line. Each unit has four variable-pitch blades 6.55 feet in diameter driven by an AE1 1,000hp electric motor controlled directly from the bridge. Steel flush-mounted hydraulically operated tunnel doors preserve the streamlining of the hull when the thrusters are not in use.

The semibalanced rudder, which weighs 75 tons, was manufactured in

At each drydocking the anchors and chains are lowered out on to the dock for inspection. Each chain is 1,080 feet long and made up of 90-foot lengths. The joining shackle of each length is painted white to identify the amount that is to be used when the ship is at anchor.

In the spring of 1987, the *Queen* was afloat once more. The new engines have been installed, and the modified funnel replaced. Temporary roofing over the after decks provides protection from Europe's cold winters while workers continue to modify the accommodations.

Norway by A/S Strommens Vaerksted. It is controlled by a four-ram electro hydraulic steering gear supplied by Brown Brothers of Edinburgh. Although one is sufficient, it has two pumping units. Under normal conditions the steering gear is operated automatically from the bridge, but in an emergency the rudder can be controlled from a position local to the machinery.

The Denny-Brown AEG stabilizers were manufactured by Brown Brothers. Each of the four retractable fins has an area of 70 square feet. Fully extended, they protrude about 12 feet from the ship's side. When not in use or when entering port, the fins are hinged forward into recesses in the ship's hull. All four fins are controlled from a central point but are hydraulically independent of one another and are fully automatic in action. In use, the stabilizers work in pairs, on each side of the ship, pivoting in opposite directions to counteract the roll.

Passive resistance to the rolling motion is present in the form of bilge keels, which are fixed to the turn of the hull on each side of the ship.

The re-engining of the *QE2* was continually supervised by the Cunard Line team of shore-based staff and, most important, by the shipboard engineer officers who take the ship to sea. The ship's officers come under the leadership of the chief engineer, whose responsibilities are far-reaching and rarely fully appreciated by the crew, not to mention the passengers. The achievements of his department are more often overshadowed by the grandeur of the ship. His expertise, and those of the design engineers, led to the successful completion of yet another episode in the continuing technical challenge that the Atlantic Ocean has provided since Samuel Cunard's first pioneering voyage of the *Britannia* in 1840.

CHAPTER NINE

Into a New Era

The *QE2*'s return to service in April 1987 coincided with an important accolade to the company: The Queen's Award for export achievement was presented to the Cunard Line. Presenting the award, Field Marshall the Lord Bramall, the lord-lieutenant of Greater London, said: "Cunard was selected for this honor because the company has not only generated and sustained a significant increase in overseas income, especially from the United States, but has achieved it in an industry noted for over-capacity and ferocious competition."

On April 29, the Princess of Wales made her first visit to the *Queen Elizabeth 2* when she embarked off Cowes, on the Isle of Wight, to join a party of more than 400 schoolchildren from the Southampton area who had boarded the ship at the dock. During her tour of the ship, Princess Diana visited the bridge and sounded the ship's whistle—as Prince Charles had done in the Clyde nineteen years before. There was a fly-pass by the *Concorde* and a display of R.A.F. Harrier jets. While on board Princes Diana unveiled a silver plaque commemorating her visit, which is on display by the "G" stairway on the Upper Deck.

The month of May saw the North Atlantic gales initiate the newly commissioned *QE2* on her way back from her first trip to New York since the engine conversion. The storm, with winds up to fifty knots and forty-foot seas, was encountered during the evening and was unexpected. As a result there was considerable damage, especially in the kitchens, where racks of china broke adrift. In the lounge, the piano and numerous items of furniture were over-

QE2 carried a message for the citizens of New York as she steamed up the Hudson River into her berth on the west side of Manhattan. On this occasion, four Moran tugs were required to assist her to dock against strong tides. (Photo courtesy of Francis J. Duffy.)

Shortly after docking in New York, a bunker barge is positioned alongside the *Queen* to replenish the supply of oil fuel used during a transatlantic crossing. Over 4,500 tons of fuel can be kept in various tanks along the bottom of the ship. (Photo courtesy of J. R. Murphy.)

turned. It was one of the worst crossings in years, and, not surprisingly, the ship arrived at her destination several hours late.

A new United States Customs policy subjecting all vessels and airplanes coming from Colombia to intensive searches caused many of the passengers and crew of the *QE2* consternation when she arrived at Los Angeles on January 28, 1988. A six-hour search for drugs delayed the disembarkation and postponed crew leave for hours while five trained dogs ran through the ship and sniffed luggage on the quay belonging to the 1,265 passengers.

Captain Alan Bennell had the honor of entertaining Her Majesty Queen Elizabeth, the Queen Mother, for lunch on board in Southampton on Decem-

The layout of the after decks has changed on a number of occasions throughout the life of the ship. In 1994, the Quarter Deck swimming pool, the Magrodome roof, and the two large tenders were removed to create the Lido and to give additional external deck space.

ber 14, 1988. The occasion was to celebrate the fiftieth anniversary of Her Majesty's launching the *Queen Elizabeth* at Clydebank, Scotland, on September 27, 1938.

To celebrate the 130th anniversary of the city of Yokohama, a consortium of Japanese companies chartered the *Queen Elizabeth 2* for seventy-two days. The charter commenced on March 27, 1989, and the ship docked alongside the passenger terminal in the port as a central attraction. Although she did not go to sea, she maintained her status as an ocean liner throughout her stay. Every day several hundred visitors arrived to spend the night aboard and another 1,200 or so would just spend a few hours having lunch, looking around, or shopping. All the usual events took place—the bars, casino, swimming pools, beauticians, and shops were open, and there was a full program of entertainment. The atmosphere was kept Western, but it was supplemented by Japanese staff, with signs and menus translated into Japanese. The authorities permitted wedding ceremonies to be carried out on board, but not by the captain. In December the *QE2* returned to Japan for a similar six-month charter for the World Exposition in Osaka. After Expo, the ship made short cruises to Hong Kong and other nearby ports.

Under the command of Captain Robin Woodall, R.D., R.N.R., in July 1990 the ship made her fastest-ever eastbound crossing of the Atlantic Ocean. Her average speed was 30.16 knots in four days, six hours, and fifty-seven minutes—ninety-nine minutes less than the previous fastest passage.

To commemorate 150 years of achievement and to mark the maiden voyage of the *Britannia* in 1840, Cunard planned a series of special voyages and cruises in 1990. The most colorful cruise began from Southampton on July 22, when the *Queen* sailed for Cóbh, Liverpool, Greenock, and Cherbourg.

About 60,000 people turned out to greet the ship when she sailed into Cóbh at dawn on July 23. It was the first time the *QE2* had docked in the Irish port. She berthed at the new Ringaskiddy container terminal, which was then officially opened by the Irish premier, Charles Haughey. After the ceremony, the premier joined Captain Woodall and other distinguished guests for a reception on board.

When the *Queen Elizabeth 2* arrived at Liverpool the following day on her first visit ever, she received the most spectacular of welcomes. Hundreds of thousands of spectators cheering and waving banners from the riverbanks and a flotilla of boats of many shapes and sizes greeted the *QE2* as she approached her anchorage. Throughout the day people came out to greet the ship and sight her from the banks of the Mersey. The *Queen* was anchored in the River Mersey near the spot where the paddle steamer *Britannia* had sailed on her historical maiden voyage to Boston and Halifax 150 years before. An inaugural party was held on deck shortly before noon, and to mark the occasion 10,000 balloons were released from the Quarter Deck swimming pool.

The port of Liverpool always gives the *Queen* a very warm reception, and as an acknowledgment, on this occasion, thousands of balloons were released from the after deck as the ship bid farewell to the city on her way down the River Mersey. (Photo courtesy of Ocean Pictures.)

Many of the crew had gathered together in the Magrodome* the previous evening and worked well into the night inflating the balloons. The port of Liverpool bade farewell to the liner amid a spectacular fireworks display and the twinkling flashes of light from thousands of cameras.

The nostalgic arrival at Greenock on July 25 marked the first return of the *Queen* to Scotland since she was launched in 1967. Again she was greeted by thousands gathered at every vantage point as she docked to the sounds of the Strathclyde Police Pipe Band.

When the *QE2* sailed from Cherbourg on July 26, Captain Ronald W. Warwick was in command, having taken over from the senior master, Captain Woodall, in order to release him for the events of the following day. This event was another historic occasion in the Cunard Line because it was the first time that a Cunard master had captained the same ship as his father.

The climax of the 150th anniversary year celebrations took place in the Solent on July 27, 1990. This was the royal revue of Cunard and Royal Naval ships at Spit Head by Her Majesty Queen Elizabeth II from H.M.Y. *Britannia*. The royal yacht was lead by T.H.V. *Patricia*, with the Elder Brethren of

*Now the Lido Restaurant.

Her Majesty Queen Elizabeth II listens with interest to Captain Warwick on the bridge during her visit commemorating the 150th anniversary year of Cunard Line. Cunard Line's senior master, Captain Robin Woodall R. D., R.N.R. (right) talks with His Royal Highness, the Prince Philip while he inspects the steering wheel. (Photo courtesy of Ocean Pictures.)

Trinity House lining her quarter-deck. The long-standing tradition of the Elder Brethren escorting the monarch while in pilotage waters was started by King George IV in 1822. (The corporation has been closely associated with the royal yachts since 1660.) The parade of ships was followed by a fly-past of the *Concorde*, a Britannia B747, a Virgin Atlantic B707, Sea Harrier aircraft, and the Trafalgar House Dauphine helicopter, which had been carried on the deck of the *QE2* for the cruise.

Shortly before noon the royal yacht stopped nearby, and Her Majesty and H.R.H. Prince Philip transferred by tender to the *QE2*. As Her Majesty stepped on board, her personal standard was broken out at the mast truck to indicate her presence on board. Sir Nigel Broakes, chairman of Trafalgar House, and Captain Woodall were at the gangway to meet the royal party and to escort them to the Queen's Room for a reception. Her Majesty the Queen then went into the Grand Lounge to unveil a plaque commemorating her visit on board. As the queen made her way to the Columbia Restaurant,* she took time to speak with passengers. During lunch the *QE2* weighed anchor and, led by T.H.V. *Patricia*, slowly cruised toward the docks. Her Majesty arrived on the bridge in time to witness the liner she launched and named after herself in 1967 dock gently alongside the terminal.

When the *QE2* arrived at New York from Southampton on August 9, 1990, she had completed her 500th scheduled transatlantic crossing since she came

*Now renamed Caronia.

The highlight of the 150th anniversary year celebrations in 1990 was the royal review in Southampton. The royal yacht *Britannia*, bearing the same name as Samuel Cunard's first ship, sails past the *QE2* as she lies majestically at anchor in the River Solent. (Photo courtesy of Glyn Genin.)

into service. At an average speed of 28 $^1/_2$ knots the crossing takes about four and a half days, depending on the route taken. The weather forecast and reports of the presence of icebergs in the region of the Grand Banks of Newfoundland will have a bearing on which course is set. If the ice has drifted well to the south, an extra hundred and fifty miles could be added to the overall distance.

On August 20, 1990, the *QE2* was heading against gale-force winds for the North Sea on the first day of the Norwegian cruise. Shortly after midday, the chief radio officer informed Captain Warwick that the automatic radio receiver had picked up the international distress signal MAYDAY from the accommodation platform West Gamma. The message said the rig was adrift with forty-nine people on board, the helicopter landing platform was damaged, some lifesaving appliances had been destroyed, and the rig was in danger of capsizing. They requested immediate assistance. A few minutes later the situation was confirmed by the Danish Coast Guard, and the *QE2* altered course for the distress area, forty-seven miles away. Although proceeding at full speed, the *QE2* was still battling against high seas and Force-9 winds. It

When the *QE2* went to Germany for repairs in 1992, she was comfortably accommodated in one of the largest floating dry docks in the world, which is situated on the river in the heart of the city of Hamburg. (Photo courtesy of Ian Denton.)

was not until two hours and eighteen minutes later that the rig was sighted in the overcast sky ahead. By this time, rescue helicopters and other vessels had appeared on the scene. On arrival, the *QE2* was put in charge of the rescue operations, but soon after the captain of the rig informed Captain Warwick that they had their situation under control and did not wish to be evacuated. The rig captain then released the *QE2* from the obligation to stand by and passage to Bergen, Norway, was resumed. It was reported that the West Gamma did capsize later that same night. Fortunately, all crew were rescued from the sea by helicopters.

Rounding off the 150th celebration year, the *QE2* made calls to Halifax and Boston—the first ports visited by the paddle steamer *Britannia* in 1840. Governor Michael Dukakis of Massachusetts declared September 4 "Cunard Day" throughout the state in honor of the company's anniversary.

The year 1990 came to a close when the *QE2* proceeded to Hamburg for her refitting in December. The shipyard selected to carry out the work was Blohm & Voss, located in the heart of the city. The ship entered one of the largest floating dry docks in the world and, within a few hours of arrival, was lifted out of the water. In addition to major overhaul of the hull and machinery, the

During a world cruise the *QE2* lies peacefully at anchor in the tranquillity of the Tahitian Islands. The ship's tenders lay alongside ready to ferry passengers ashore.

casino was extended and remodeled to the designs of Graham Faye and a new restaurant, the Princess Grill Starboard,* was added.

Meanwhile, in Malta, the *Cunard Princess* was chartered by the United States Army for service in the Persian Gulf. The cruise ship, under the command of Captain Keith Stanley, was based in Bahrain as a rest and recreation facility for U.S. troops involved in Operation Desert Storm. Every three days, 850 soldiers went aboard and enjoyed all the facilities available to passengers on a cruise, in particular hot showers and cold beer. There were only two differences: there was no casino, and the ship never sailed. During the time in Bahrain, General Norman Schwarzkopf visited the *Cunard Princess* and paid tribute to the crew. Later the ship was issued a certificate of commendation for Outstanding Performance and Meritorious Service. Some 50,000 troops had spent time on board.

His Royal Highness, the Prince Edward, made his debut on board the *Queen Elizabeth 2* on June 15, 1991, when he attended the *QE2* Royal Ball with

*Now named Britannia Grill.

his father, the Duke of Edinburgh. The prince is chairman of the Duke of Edinburgh's Award Special Projects Group.

Shortly after the *QE2* returned from her 1992 world cruise, a celebration was held on board to commemorate the tenth anniversary of the Falkland Campaign. The guest of honor for the luncheon was the Right Honorable Margaret Thatcher, O.M., F.R.S. In a speech after lunch, Sir Nigel Broakes welcomed Mrs. Thatcher and said the company was pleased that the *QE2* had been able to be of service in the campaign. In response, Mrs. Thatcher gave a stirring speech in which she spoke of the events leading up to the war and emphasized the importance of the *QE2*'s participation in it.

Misfortune came to the *QE2* on a cruise a few months later when she was sailing westerly along Vineyard Sound off the New England coast, near Martha's Vineyard, bound for New York. Shortly before 2200 hours on August 7, when passing south of Cuttyhunk Island, the captain, pilot, and officers on the bridge felt a rumbling, heavy vibrations, and the ship shaking. The captain's first reaction was that the ship had struck a floating object or that there was a problem in the engine room. These thoughts were quickly eliminated. The least-expected conclusion was that the ship must have struck an uncharted object or rocks on the sea bed. Captain Woodall immediately stopped the ship and ordered some of the crew to emergency stations to inspect for possible damage. The chief engineer soon reported that the steering gear and propulsion machinery were not affected and remained in full working order.

From other parts of the ship it was reported that the vibration was hardly noticeable or not even felt. Some passengers seated for dinner noticed a slight tremor, but it was not enough to stop a group of waiters in one of the restaurants from singing happy anniversary to a celebrating couple. There was no panic, and most people were untroubled by the incident. The evening's cabaret continued, the musicians played on, and the roulette wheel kept spinning in the casino.

Meanwhile, information was received on the bridge that there was water in some of the double-bottom tanks that should have been empty. It was concluded that two fresh-water and one saltwater ballast and an empty fuel tank had been breached. Calculations established that the stability of the ship was not in any danger and that any ingress of water could be adequately taken care of with the water ballast pumps.

As a formality, the captain notified the United States Coast Guard by radio and was informed by them that the liner must anchor nearby for further investigation until they were satisfied that there was no danger to passengers or a threat of oil pollution to the environment. These procedures took a long time, and the *Queen* had to remain where she was until 1700 hours the following day.

On hearing the news, Cunard Line personnel in New York swung into action to prepare for a mass disembarkation of passengers. Obtaining transport at short notice over the weekend was no easy task. Bob Murphy, owner of Saddle River Tours, saw the report on CNN and telephoned the head office offering to send five buses from as far away as New Jersey, which were gratefully accepted. Local ferry boats were chartered to take some passengers ashore to Newport, where they were met by bus and transferred to trains for onward travel to New York. The baggage was discharged from the ship when it arrived at Boston and was sent to the owners by air. The *QE2* arrived in Boston the following Monday and later entered the dry dock.

An inspection of the hull commenced as soon as all the water was pumped out of the dry dock. The damaged area was found to be mainly confined to the forward section of the ship near the keel, where the steel is one and one-half inches thick and constructed to withstand the inclement elements of the North Atlantic in the winter. A series of intermittent gashes were sighted up to seventy-four feet long and three inches wide running in various areas between the bow and amidships. The after part of the ship, including the propellers and rudder, were unscathed. Temporary repairs, which included welding over of the small cracks and fitting steel patches over the larger ones, were carried out by the General Ship Corporation of Boston. Meanwhile, after inviting bids from several shipyards in the United States and Europe, Cunard chose Blohm & Voss to carry out the permanent repairs.

As a result of the accident, the first survey in fifty-three years of Vineyard Sound was carried out by the National Oceanic and Atmospheric Administration (NOAA). The NOAA survey discovered the presence of uncharted rocks in the position of the incident and other previously uncharted ridges in the seabed in the general area.

The repairs were completed by October 4, and the *Queen* resumed service for a brief period with a cruise from Southampton. By the end of the following month, she had returned to Hamburg once again to have one of the engines replaced. This work was scheduled long before the incident at Martha's Vineyard, but the replacement engine was still under construction at the time of the hull repairs.

Both the dry dock periods provided an opportunity to carry out further upgrades of the internal accommodations. This included refurbishment of the movie theater and the commencement of a major redesign and rebuilding of the Spa at Sea. By mid-December the *Queen* was back in service on the Atlantic heading for New York and the 1993 world cruise.

At the home office, the parent company, Trafalgar House, was having to contend with Cunard's profit performance, which was suffering from the downturn of the economy that affected most of the cruise industry. This coincided with an announcement that Hong Kong Land had acquired 14.9 percent of the share capital of Trafalgar House. Hong Kong Land eventually increased their holding to give them effective control of the company, under

The 37,845-ton *Royal Viking Sun* was built in Finland, came into service in 1988, and was acquired by Cunard Line in 1994. With a capacity for 814 passengers and a crew of 740, she is usually engaged on long-distance cruising and is seen here transiting the Panama Canal. The *Royal Viking Sun* will be renamed *Seabourn Sun* after her refit toward the end of 1999.

the chairmanship of Simon Keswick. Not deterred, Cunard entered into an agreement with Crown Cruise Line (owned by the Finnish company EffJohn International) to manage their three new ships: *Crown Monarch*, *Crown Jewel*, and *Crown Dynasty*. The ships were consolidated with the *Cunard Countess* and the *Cunard Princess* to form the Cunard Crown Line.

The *QE2* carried an unusual cargo in the forward hold when she sailed on a transatlantic crossing from New York on August 14, 1993. She had on board a Tiger Moth aircraft, accompanied by its owner; Roger Fiennes. The aircraft had been flown around various parts of the United States at air ralleys and had a well-documented flying history. Some five years later, in April 1998, Fiennes took off from Dieppe heading for the English Channel and has never been seen since.

Hundreds of vessels gathered off Spit Head on June 5 for the celebration of the fiftieth anniversary of the D-Day landings. The Royal Yacht *Britannia* was at the heart of the fleet, but she was dwarfed by the *Queen Elizabeth 2* and the U.S. aircraft carrier *George Washington* as dozens of small craft swirled around, carving white lines in the Solent with their wake. On board the *QE2*, passengers and war veterans were entertained by Dame Vera Lynn and Bob Hope as the ship sailed across the Channel on her remembrance voyage.

Two cruise lines with proud traditions of excellence came together on June 30, 1994, when Cunard purchased the luxury cruise ship *Royal Viking Sun* for $170 million. The vessel was built in Helsinki, Finland, and since she came into service in 1988 she has been annually recognized by the *Berlitz Complete Guide to Cruising & Cruise Ships* as the highest-rated cruise ship in the world. The acquisition of this fine vessel was a major step forward in the plans of the new management of Trafalgar House and Cunard Line in their stated determination to rebuild the passenger fleet. It also gave a strong signal to the industry observers who had for a long time doubted Trafalgar House's commitment to the shipping business. By the following October, there was word on the waterfront that the Cunard management agreement with Crown Cruise Line was in jeopardy. The partnership was gradually dissolved and followed by the demise of other ships in the fleet.

Heavy weather and darkness is never far away when distress calls are received on the North Atlantic. Such was the case on October 5, 1994, when Captain Woodall diverted the *Queen* 120 miles to help save the life of seriously ill crew member Harry Brooks, 43, on the fishing vessel *Gail Ann*. As the captain prepared to maneuver his ship, he warned passengers that he would be stopping the engines and that, with the stabilizers withdrawn, the liner was likely to move uncomfortably in the heavy northerly swell. Hundreds of passengers were out on deck to watch as the unconscious seaman was transferred across turbulent seas to recover in the medical facilities of the *QE2*. When Brooks regained consciousness he had no idea of what had taken place, and it took a while for the hospital staff to convince him that he was on board the *Queen* bound for England.

The end of October saw the retirement of Captain Robin Woodall. He was one of the most experienced captains in the company and had the rare distinction of being one of few officers who had spent his entire forty-four years at sea with the Cunard Line. He was a second officer on the maiden voyage of the *QE2* and was given his first command of the liner in November 1987. Captain Woodall kept a meticulous diary of his seagoing career. When he retired on October 30, he had sailed 3,247,918 miles.

Early in the year Cunard had announced that $45 million was to be spent on a much-needed major refurbishment of the *QE2*. Blohm & Voss won the contract to carry out the work, and MET Studio Ltd. and John McNeece Ltd. were appointed interior designers. By coincidence, Alex McCuaig, managing director of MET Studio, began his career working with James Gard-

At the approach to the Caronia Restaurant, the large and spectacular model of the *Mauretania* provides a centerpiece to the Heritage Trail. The Heritage Trail was created in 1994 as a testament to the pride with which the Cunard Line regards the traditions and distinguished history of the company. (Photo courtesy of Alan Chandler.)

ner, one of the original design coordinators of the *QE2*. John McNeece has more than thirty years' experience in the design of cruise ship interiors, which includes the redesign of cabins and public rooms on the *Cunard Countess* and *Cunard Princess*.

The designers were asked to produce a master plan to reintroduce a coordinated design throughout the ship, with particular reference to the use of fabrics and color schemes that had become fragmented or lost over the years due to numerous piecemeal changes. They were required to make the public areas more comfortable and as multifunctional as possible, giving special attention to the flow and movement of passengers on the ship. The cabin bathrooms had to be replaced to bring them up to modern-day standards. Life was given to the stairways, achieved by introducing artwork, wooden paneling, and handrails. One of the most popular improvements was the introduction of the museum-style exhibition of history around the ship. Known as the Heritage Trail, it features ephemera, memorabilia, ship models, and artifacts from earlier voyages and past ships and is designed to focus on Cunard's illustrious maritime history. Other small but essential features, such as renewing all the clocks and signage throughout the ship, had to be considered. Designs had to be created for a new informal buffet-style restaurant located at the after end of the Quarter Deck in place of the Magradome and swimming pool. This presented a challenge to the designers as there was a requirement for it to be spacious and efficient and at the same time have an acceptable ambiance for use in the evening and the traditional midnight buffet. Externally, the dark gray hull was replaced by royal blue and the tricolor stripe added to the superstructure.

A limited amount of bathroom and cabin refurbishment commenced during the summer voyages. On November 13, after disembarking all her passengers, the ship went out of service and headed for Europe with contractors and workers on board. Shortly after arriving in Hamburg on November 20, the *QE2* entered dry dock and work began in earnest. When the ship arrived back in Southampton twenty-five days later, some of the refurbishment had not been completed. Although work continued around the clock, it soon became apparent that the liner would not be ready before the scheduled sailing time. Notwithstanding, the *Queen* departed for New York with a valid passenger certificate issued by the Marine Safety Agency. The certificate restricted the number of passengers that could be carried to 1,000 instead of the usual 1,900 due to the unfinished work. Arrangements were made for work to continue during the ocean passage, but the ship encountered one of the worst gales of the year as soon as she cleared the western approaches to the English Channel. The productivity of many of the workmen was considerably reduced, and some were unable to carry out the tasks that they remained on board to complete.

The difficulties associated with the outstanding work were well documented by the media but in some instances the reports did not represent the true status of the ship, her crew, or passengers. What was generally overlooked was the vast amount of impressive redesign work that was finished on schedule. Douglas Ward, author of the *Berlitz Guide*, made an unannounced inspection of the *Queen* ten days after she sailed from Southampton and wrote:

> The refurbishment has converted the ship into a classic, majestic vessel, with an interior reminiscent of the greatest ocean liners ever built.

Elsewhere in the fleet, the *Cunard Princess*, after eighteen years of service, was being handed over to her new owners, the Mediterranean Shipping Company at Naples, Italy, on April 26, 1995. Before leaving the ship, Captain Warwick had the Cunard crest removed from the bow, and he had it mounted on the bridge front of the *QE2* when he returned there the following September.

The first-ever around-Britain cruise of the *Queen* was made in September 1995 and turned out to be a family affair for Captain Warwick, who was joined for the voyage by his father. It was also a reunion for other former mas-

Chef Jonathon Wicks and Captain Warwick's wife, Kim, look on as the captain cuts a cake presented to the ship by a bakery in Liverpool. It may have been a bad omen to have made the first cut across the bow because a week later the ship encountered a 90-foot rogue wave as she crossed the North Atlantic Ocean. (Photo courtesy of Ocean Pictures.)

ters: Captains Mortimer Hehir, Robert Arnott, and Robin Woodall and the late Commodore Geoffrey T. Marr, D.S.O., R.D., all of whom visited the ship during the voyage, which included a return visit to Liverpool. To commemorate the visit to Liverpool, a well-known city bakery presented the ship with a large fruit cake in the form of a model of the *QE2*. While everyone thought it would be nice to keep the cake, the chef recommended that it be consumed. Accordingly, it was decided that it would be served with afternoon tea in the Queen's Room and that the captain would be asked to cut it. This presented him with a dilemma—where should the first cut be made on such a work of art? After a lot of debate with those in attendance, the captain chose to cut the bow off. This decision may have been a bad omen for the following voyage.

When the *QE2* sailed from Southampton on September 7, 1995, bound for Cherbourg, there was some doubt as to whether she would be able to dock due to the proximity of Hurricane Iris. Luck was with the ship when the arrival coincided with a period of calm as the eye of the storm passed over the vicinity of the port. The same could not be said for the next leg of the voyage.

After clearing Bishop's Rock early on the morning of September 8, 1995, a great circle course was set for New York via Cape Race, on the south coast of Newfoundland. During the ocean passage the weather in the North Atlantic is monitored regularly by the officers on watch. Accordingly, the movement of Hurricane Luis in the Caribbean was being plotted. As the hurricane left the Caribbean area it became apparent that there was a chance that it would pass close to the course of the *Queen*. On September 10 the great circle course was abandoned and the course altered to southwesterly to increase the distance from the predicted path of the storm, which was estimated to pass ahead of the *QE2* at 2300 hours that evening. Captain Warwick informed the passengers of the proximity of Luis and told them that they could expect to feel the effects of the storm sometime after dinner. He also warned them of the danger of going out on decks as the wind became stronger. At the same time, the crew was ordered to prepare for unfavorable weather conditions. By the time dinner was over on Sunday evening, the winds had strengthened to more than 50 knots. The wind force was to become far greater than forecast. Despite the storm being more than 140 miles away the wind reached a recorded speed of over 100 knots. The strength of the wind caused the ship to list seven degrees when it was on the port beam of the liner. By this time Luis was making a forward speed estimated to be between 40 and 50 knots. As it headed northeasterly, the wind direction soon started to move from the port beam to the bow, and the ship began to encounter heavy head seas. At the same time it became necessary to start reducing the speed of the ship and by 0145 hours on Monday morning the *QE2* was hove to and riding out waves of 30 to 40 feet.

It was a dark night, and the visibility was considerably affected by the storm conditions. The sea was nearly white in appearance, with foam and driving spray lashing the ship. Waves were continuously breaking over the fore deck, leaving it awash for minutes at a time. At 0210 hours a large wave was sighted right ahead looming out of the darkness. The wave seemed to take ages to reach the ship, but it was probably less than a minute before it broke with tremendous force over the bow of the *Queen*. A shudder went through the ship. The sea cascaded all over the forward deck, including the bridge, and it was several seconds before the water had drained away from the wheelhouse windows and the vision ahead restored.

The weight of the water landing on the foredeck bent a few of the railings and dented the deck plating. Many of the passengers slept through the rogue wave and only became aware of it when they were given a Storm Certificate the next day.

Sometimes it can be quite difficult to gauge wave height in a storm, but in this case the crest of the wave was more or less level with the line of sight on the bridge, which is at a height of 95 feet above the sea surface. The presence of the rogue wave was also recorded by Canadian weather buoys moored in the vicinity, which measured the height as 98 feet.

Cunard cruised into deep water toward the end of 1995 when further losses were reported by Trafalgar House, but with the introduction of new management, the company remained committed to hold up against any adversary. By the following spring, the Norwegian company Kvaerner had declared their interest in acquiring Trafalgar House for their construction and engineering elements and for a base to establish their headquarters in London. By April the whole company was sold to Kvaerner for £904 million. From the onset of talks between the two companies it was made clear that Trafalgar House would not split up the group, so the purchase had to include Cunard, even though it would become a non-core asset in the new owner's group. This immediately gave rise to speculation that Cunard was up for sale. For months after, the media reported numerous prospective purchasers for the *QE2* and the other ships in the fleet. Among the reported contenders were Vlasov, Carnival, P & O, Disney, Virgin, Prudential, and Cruise Holdings; there was even a proposal to use the *QE2* as a hotel complex on a small island in the South Pacific.

The *Cunard Countess*, the younger sister ship of the *Cunard Princess*, was sold on November 12, 1996, to the Awani Shipping Company and went on to sail in Indonesian waters. The sale of this popular vessel and her predecessor, the *Cunard Adventurer*, in 1977 signaled the end of more than twenty-five years of continuous Cunard presence in the eastern Caribbean. In addition to providing cruises for hundreds of thousands of vacationers, there is no doubt that the all-year-round itineraries of the two cruise ships helped to influence the growth of tourism and the cruise industry in the islands they visited. In April, less than six months later, the *Sagafjord* was sold to Saga Holidays and renamed *Sagarose*. The following month saw the handing over of the *Crown Dynasty* to sever the final link with Crown Cruise Line.

One of the major changes in 1997 from previous years, largely resulting from passenger demand, was the extending of the five-day transatlantic crossing of the *Queen* to six days. This not only allows passengers more leisure time at sea but gives the ship flexibility to pursue a more southerly route should weather conditions demand it.

Burials at sea are uncommon these days, but from time to time the scattering of ashes still takes place from the decks of the *Queen Elizabeth 2*. Such was the case in mid-Atlantic on April 14, 1997, when the ashes of Commodore Geoffrey T. Marr were committed to the deep by Captain Roland Hasell. Commodore Marr sailed in command of the *Queen Mary* and the *Queen Elizabeth* before he retired in 1968.

Early in 1997 arrangements began to be put in place to mark the thirtieth anniversary of the launching of the *QE2* by hosting a benefit lunch in aid of land mine victims with Diana, Princess of Wales, as the guest of honor. Fol-

The cliffs of the Norwegian Fjords tower above the *Queen* in the early morning mist as she lies at anchor. (Photo courtesy of Gerald Brimacombe.)

lowing the tragic death of the princess, Cunard and the British Red Cross decided to go ahead with the event as a tribute to her crusade against land mines. The event was hosted on board by the chairman of Cunard, Antti Pankakoski, and Captain Warwick. The tributes to Princess Diana were led by Lord Attenborough and Elizabeth Dole, president of the American Red Cross. Cherie Blair, wife of the prime minister, and Terry Waite were also in attendance.

Several months later, the *Queen Elizabeth 2* was honored to host another important charity during the 1998 world cruise, under the command of Captain Warwick. When the *Queen* arrived at Durban on March 29, South African President Nelson Mandela embarked with his companion, Mrs. Graça Machel, for an historic voyage to Cape Town. Shortly after the president's arrival on board, he and Zulu Chief Mangosuthu Buthelezi, South Africa's Home Affairs minister, were interviewed by Sir David Frost. The interview was beamed live from South Africa to the U.K. and shown on BBC's *Breakfast with Frost* program. In Cape Town the liner was the venue for a charity dinner and auction sale to raise funds for the Nelson Mandela Children's Fund.

As the *Queen Elizabeth 2* headed north in the South Atlantic the captain received the good news that Kvaerner had sold the Cunard Line to the Miami-

Even the giant *QE2* looks small as she lies at anchor in Geiranger Fjord surrounded by some of the most spectacular scenery in the world. (Photo courtesy of Gerald Brimacombe.)

based Carnival Corporation for $500 million. Simultaneously, a merger was completed between Cunard and Seabourn Cruise Line, the latter having been equally owned by Carnival and Mr. Atle Brynested. The Carnival Corporation now owns a 68 percent share of the newly merged company, named Cunard Line, Ltd., with the balance being held by Brynestad and a group of Norwegian investors. Other companies owned by the Carnival Corporation include Carnival Cruise Line, Holland America Line, and Windstar Cruises; they also have substantial equity interests in Costa Cruises and Airtours Plc. After twenty-five years as a small division in a conglomerate, half a decade of fragmented management and speculation, the *Queen Elizabeth 2*, the world's best-known ship, is back in the playing field as part of the world's leading cruise ship company.

The *Queen Elizabeth 2* has traveled more than four and a quarter million miles and visited 251 different places around the world during the more than 30 years since she was launched on September 20, 1967. She attracts the attention of the world in unique ways that are not shared by other ships. She

Colorful small boats enliven the scene as the *Queen Elizabeth 2* lies at anchor against the grandeur of the mountains on her annual cruise to Norway. (Photo courtesy of Gerald Brimacombe.)

continues to sail oceans, seas, and rivers around the globe, carrying nearly 2,000 passengers and a crew of 1,000 at a speed in excess of 30 miles an hour in the height of luxury. When she went into service in 1969 she was a supreme feat of British technology and revolutionary in many ways. Today, three decades later, she remains technically modern, and continued efforts will be made to keep her so. Her voyages have taken her through many contrasts of cultures and civilizations. Every journey is different, memorable, and important in one way or another to those who sail on board her.

The *QE2* has become a legend before she becomes a memory and, as such, sails on, carrying the flag of the world's first and oldest transatlantic steamship company. As part of Britain's maritime heritage she is the most majestic and sophisticated passenger liner ever built and bears testimony to the traditions that Cunard signifies: luxury, elegance, life enrichment, and international friendship.

The *Queen Elizabeth 2* remains a living memory and monument to the founder, Sir Samuel Cunard.

CHAPTER TEN

Guide to the *Queen Elizabeth 2*

The guide to the *QE2*, starting on the uppermost deck, working down, and forward to aft on each deck, describes the *QE2* as she presently exists with the various alterations that have been made since she first went into service in 1969. The majority of changes were incorporated to upgrade the standard of passenger life on board. Other alterations, such as those to accommodate the health spa, Computer Learning Centre, and Lido Restaurant, reflect the trends of modern living.

The Mast
After the funnel, the top of the mast is the highest part of the ship, being 169 feet, 1 inch above the waterline when the draft is 31 feet. Because the aerial for the satellite navigation system was situated at the top, the mast was 5 feet higher when the ship was commissioned. This aerial was removed when the satellite receiver was updated. Unlike the old liners, the *QE2* does not have a crow's nest, but there is access to the navigation lights and whistles provided by a forty-foot ladder inside the mast. Part of the mast also acts as a duct to ventilate air from the kitchens.

Various flags are flown at different times on the mast. The national flag, known as the courtesy ensign, of the country being visited is flown at the highest point. The Cunard House flag and signal flags are hoisted on the starboard and port yardarms. When the vessel is under way, the British ensign is flown from the gaff. The ensign is usually red, but if the captain is a Royal Naval Reserve officer he can fly the blue ensign if he so desires.

A closed circuit television camera is installed on the mast, which is directed

The mast of the *QE2* towers 200 feet, 1 inch above the keel of the liner, and 169 feet, 1 inch above the waterline, when the *Queen* is drawing her normal 31-foot draft. Next to the funnel, the top of the mast is the highest part of the ship.

astern. This enables the engineer officer on watch in the Engine Control Room to monitor the engine exhaust from the funnel.

The Funnel

The funnel, 204 feet, $1\frac{1}{2}$ inches above the keel, is 4 feet higher than the mast and from an external view probably the most noticeable feature of the *QE2*. The original black-and-white color scheme of the funnel was a breakaway from Cunard tradition, but at the time it was felt that red with black bands (the Cunard colors) would not look appropriate with the modern functional design. However, in 1982, when the hull color was changed to a very light gray, the funnel was painted in Cunard colors and remained as such when the hull was sprayed again in 1983 to dark gray. In 1994 the hull was painted to the present-day dark blue.

The design of the funnel was the result of many months of research carried out by Cunard's technical department and wind-tunnel tests at the National

The area aft of the funnel on Sports Deck is usually referred to as the "helicopter deck." This photograph would have been taken during a chilly transatlantic crossing when the deck stewards traditionally turn the chairs to face the sun and provide passengers with thick blankets and warm drinks at their request. (Photo courtesy of Robin Ebers.)

173

Physical Laboratory at Teddington, Middlesex. With so much open deck space on the *QE2*, it is paramount that fumes and the occasional soot ejected from the funnel are carried well clear of the ship. To achieve this, used air from within the ship is ducted up behind the main boiler vents to create an area of high pressure and keep the exhaust up and away from the decks. In some wind conditions, however, this would not be sufficient, and the smoke would swirl back down again over the decks. To overcome this, the shovel-shaped scoop was designed and introduced to direct a stream of air up and behind the vents.

During re-engining in 1986, the funnel was removed and modified to accommodate part of the new propulsion equipment. The exterior shape is slightly wider than the original design.

Signal Deck

The Signal Deck is the highest deck on the ship. Forward, the most important area, is the bridge, consisting of the wheelhouse and chart room. The bridge of the *QE2* contains some of the most advanced navigational equipment used today, as well as more traditional equipment. In 1994 a Kelvin Hughes nucleus integrated navigation system was installed. This system enables the navigators to plot courses on electronically produced charts. The charts are provided on CD-ROM (compact disc) by the British Admiralty Hydro-

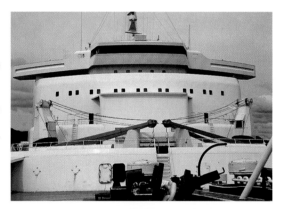

The bridge on Signal Deck sweeps across the ship from wing to wing, providing the navigating officers on duty with a clear view ahead and astern. Beneath the bridge is the Sports Deck observation area, and beneath that the long line of windows of the officers' wardroom. The white, boxlike shape in the center was added in 1972 and houses a portion of the kitchens. On either side of the Quarter Deck are the cranes. These have since been removed and replaced by a modern single unit on the port side.

graphic Office. There are three Kelvin Hughes radars. They are all daylight viewing, with a computerized facility for plotting targets automatically as well as the capability to superimpose maps on the screen when approaching harbor or coastal areas. There are Decca and Loran systems for hyperbolic navigation. Magnavox and Racal receivers are installed for the latest satellite navigation technology using the Global Positioning System (GPS). This system uses a constellation of 24 orbiting satellites to give the navigator a continuous position readout accurate to within 50 feet anywhere in the world. Other

Captain Warwick joined the Cunard Line as a junior officer in 1970. Twenty years later he commanded the *Queen Elizabeth 2* for the first time and now stands in the same spot that his father, Commodore W. E. Warwick, stood during the ship's maiden voyage in 1969.

equipment includes depth recorders, magnetic compasses, Doppler and electromagnetic speed logs, Tyfon whistles, and Sperry Gyro compasses coupled to an automatic pilot for steering. Facilities are available for receiving weather reports from meteorological stations ashore. The standard compass is situated on the roof of the bridge so that it is as far as possible from any magnetism generated by electrically operated equipment.

Consoles in the center of the bridge house controls for the variable pitch propellers, bow thrusters, steering, and stabilizers. There are numerous indicator lights and dials showing the state of the propulsion plant and the operational status of the controls. The propeller pitch, bow thruster, and steering controls are duplicated in the smaller consoles situated on each wing of the bridge.

The bridge is always manned by at least one qualified officer 24 hours of the day throughout the year. When the ship is at sea there are two officers on duty. In addition to his navigation duties, the officer on watch is responsible for the safety of the ship. In an emergency, he can close the watertight doors from the bridge. He also has direct communication with the safety control room, the engine room, and the fire equipment lockers.

The chart room is situated behind the bridge. This is mainly the navigator's domain and, as the name implies, is where all the charts are stowed when not in use. Charts are kept on board covering all the principal ocean routes and leading cruise ports of the world. Nearby is the Captain's Sea Cabin. This is a small room for his use in bad weather or in other circumstances when it is necessary to be immediately available to the bridge.

Astern of the mast is the upper level of the penthouse suites (described later), reached by a secluded elevator or stairway from either one of the two decks below. In 1987, eight more suites were added, filling in the open deck space that existed forward of the funnel base.

Farther astern are the pet kennels. This area is reached from the inside by a

The rudder, speed and bow thrusters can be operated from the consoles on each wing of the bridge. The captain and officers stand on the wings and use these controls when they are docking the ship. (Photo courtesy of Kevin Walsh.)

stairway on the starboard side of the Boat Deck, astern of the "D" stairway. There are accommodations and an exercise area on deck for eleven animals. Dogs, the most frequent travelers, are more privileged than the rest—they have their own lamp-post.

Sports Deck

Reached from the stairs leading up from each side of the Boat Deck is the foremost observation area on the Signal Deck. The whole of the foredeck can be seen from this point. A recent addition to the outboard side of the forward bulkhead is the Cunard lion crest. As mentioned earlier, the crest was originally on the bow of the *Cunard Princess*. It was put aboard the *QE2* and mounted in its present position on September 1, 1995. Immediately behind are the captain's and senior officers' quarters.

Continuing aft is the lower level of the penthouses. The penthouse accommodations did not exist when the ship was commissioned. They replaced an area of deck enclosed at the sides but open to the sky.

The penthouses were added in three stages—the first at Southampton during the1972 refitting. The suites were prefabricated ashore and then lifted on board in two halves. Each suite was given a distinctive atmosphere of its own. The two luxury units on each side forward are two-story, spanning the Signal and Sports decks, each with a private internal stairway. The port-side accommodation was named the Trafalgar Suite and was originally designed and furnished to resemble Lord Nelson's quarters on the H.M.S. *Victory*, even to the inclusion of a contemporary portrait of Lady Emma Hamilton. The starboard duplex, the Queen Anne Suite, was originally furnished in the style and period of the name it bears. Each suite has two bathrooms and private verandahs overlooking the sea. The premier Queen Mary and Queen Elizabeth suites were added when the ship was having her annual overhaul at Bayonne,

The penthouses on *QE2* are among the most spacious ever to be made available at sea. They are arranged on two decks and can be reached by a private stairway or an elevator.

The penthouse suites are attended by some of Cunard's longest and most experienced staff. Service is available twenty-four hours a day, from the moment a passenger steps on board.

New Jersey, in 1977. These two split-level suites are more luxurious than any others available at sea, and in addition to verandahs they have individual conservatories and sun decks with panoramic views forward over the bridge and ocean.

The majority of the suites are totally refurbished approximately every two years when the ship goes into refitting. Additional features subsequently fitted include whirlpool baths and video cassette players.

Continuing aft is the Children's Playroom, which was designed by Elizabeth Beloe and Tony Heaton while they were students of interior design at the Royal College of Arts. The room, staffed with an English nanny, includes a nursery for young children and a cinema with a sloping floor for those who are older. Although inboard, the room is bright and gay, with lots of colorful cupboards. The original design included curvy fiberglass screens to divide parts of the room. These have now been removed to make a larger and more attractive play area. The room is usually called Noah's Ark.

Further astern on each side of the deck are the radio and engineer officers'

The two Grande Suites, named Queen Mary and Queen Elizabeth, each consist of a bedroom with balcony, dining area, and raised lounge leading out to a conservatory and private deck area with a unique view of the forward part of the ship.

This view of the Queen Mary Suite shows the raised lounge with the bedroom beyond the dining area.

The Children's Playroom, staffed by two British nannies, is decorated along the lines of Noah's Ark and has provided an adventurous atmosphere for youngsters since the ship came into service in 1969. (Photo courtesy of Mike Moon.)

accommodations. The cabins are single berth, and each has its own adjoining bathroom.

Doorways lead out onto the open deck — commonly referred to as the "helicopter deck." The large "H" painted on the deck is a guide for helicopter pilots when making their approach.

Boat Deck
Right forward on the Boat Deck is the officers' wardroom and dining room, the windows of which look out over the foredeck. The wardroom houses a

The officers' wardroom stretches the whole width of the ship and enjoys enviable views over the fore deck. The pictures, memorabilia, and plaques presented over the years have produced a unique living history of the ship's travels. (Photo courtesy of Kevin Boag.)

An impressive indication of the internal size of the *Queen* can be seen by looking down the eight levels of the forward stairway. (Photo courtesy of Nigel Long.)

The equipment in the radio room has changed on a number of occasions over the years with the advancement of communication technology. Staff are on duty twenty-four hours a day to handle telephone calls, e-mails, and facsimile messages. (Photo courtesy of Simon Ranger.)

splendid array of nautical memorabilia collected since the ship came into service. Situated in a prominent position are signed prints of Her Majesty Queen Elizabeth II and the Duke of Edinburgh, presented in 1970. Below the prints is the original brass bell from the Cunarder R.M.S. *Aquitania*, and nearby is the engine-room telegraph of the same vessel.

On the starboard side aft of the wardroom there are accommodations for the navigating officers. The officers' duty room and one of their cabins were removed in 1987 when the Queen's Grill Restaurant was extended.

Outside the wardroom is the top of the "A" stairway. For those not put off by heights, there is an impressive view from the top all the way down to Five

The Queen's Grill Restaurant is for the exclusive use of passengers who occupy "Q" grade accommodation. All the meals served in the restaurant are prepared in the adjoining kitchen, and à la carte service is provided on transatlantic crossings.

The decor in the Queen's Grill Restaurant has changed on a number of occasions over the years but the carved wooden crest of Her Majesty Queen Elizabeth II has always been prominently displayed. (Photo courtesy of Mike Moon.)

Most of the staterooms have a sea view and feature a shower, or tub and shower, television, and satellite telephones. Some cabins are fitted with adjoining doors, making them suitable for family travel.

Deck. Nearby can be seen the *Britannia* figurehead. This was originally situated at the forward entrance to the Britannia (now Mauretania) Restaurant by "A" stairway one deck below. The figurehead is carved out of Quebec yellow pine by Cornish sculptor Charles Moore and was presented to the ship by Lloyds of London. In the square there is a large model of the steamship *Russia*, which entered service in 1867.

The Queen's Grill Bar complements the adjoining restaurant. The small intimate bar and large windows with views over the ocean provide a peaceful setting throughout the day and evening.

The Board Room on the port side of the Boat Deck has full conference facilities and is available during the voyage for passengers' use. There is direct access into the upper level of the Theatre.

The radio room is situated on the port side of the square. This department is manned 24 hours a day. The officers are constantly in touch with the outside world by radio telegraphy, telex, facsimile, e-mail, and satellite links. The ship's newspaper is received via satellite daily from the United States and Great Britain. Since the ship was launched there have been many equipment changes in the radio room reflecting advances in communication technology. In 1989 a Magnavox system was installed enabling passengers to dial direct from their cabin to virtually anywhere in the world.

Double glass doors lead from the square to the Queen's Grill Restaurant.

Known as the Royal Promenade, the shopping arcade stretches down both sides of the upper level of the Grand Lounge, covering an area that has quadrupled in size since the ship came into service. The shops offer fine designer fashions, jewelry, and gifts from many well-known manufacturers.

Captain Warwick and his father, Commodore William Warwick, share a few moments together on the bridge of the *Queen* when she called at Liverpool in 1995. This visit was a nostalgic one for the Commodore because the ship anchored in sight of the Royal Hotel, where he was born.

When the ship was commissioned, this was known as the 736 Club, the number 736 being the one given by the ship's builders to identify the "job." The *QE2* did not have a casino when she first came into service due to restrictive laws that existed in the United States. When the laws were relaxed, the 736 Club was used as the casino for a brief period before being permanently located on the Upper Deck.

At the time of the installation of the penthouses in 1972, the 736 Club was converted to the Queen's Grill Restaurant. This area has enjoyed various decors over the years, but the Queen of England's coat of arms carved out of wood has remained on the after bulkhead. The restaurant was extended to accommodate the passengers from the penthouse suites that were added in 1986. The Queen's Grill kitchen is located directly behind the restaurant and is totally dedicated to the 231 people dining there.

Doors on the starboard side lead to the Queen's Grill Lounge. This room replaces the areas once known as the Coffee Shop and the Teenage Juke Box Room. Here coffee and light meals were available throughout the day and into the night. The Juke Box Room had an area set aside for a juke box, pinball machines, and other teen playthings, such as distorting mirrors.

The Queen's Grill Lounge has also enjoyed a variety of decors. In 1982 it was remodeled along with the Queen's Grill by Dennis Lennon, the original coordinating designer of the interior of the *QE2*.

At the top of "D" stairway, Ocean Pictures, the official photographers for the Cunard Line since 1929, have a unique display, designed by Jane Hunter-Cox. A selection of various photographs taken over the years on Cunard Line

The depth of water in many of the ports around the world visited by the *Queen Elizabeth 2* is too shallow for the ship to dock. When this is the case, the ship anchors, and specially constructed tenders are used to ferry the passengers to and from shore. (Photo courtesy of Nigel Long.)

One of the two catamaran hull tenders makes her approach to the ship. Each of these tenders can carry 112 passengers and is also certified as a lifeboat.

ships can be viewed here. Opposite is the entrance to the cinema/theater balcony, which seats 136 people. After many years on loan ashore, two works of art were returned to sea in 1994 and hung on the stairway landing: portraits of Her Majesty Queen Elizabeth, the Queen Mother, and H.R.H. Princess Elizabeth and Prince Philip were originally exhibited on the *Queen Elizabeth* and the *Caronia*, respectively.

To the port side of the stairway is the Board Room, established in 1987. This replaced the Computer Learning Centre that had been installed during the 1983 refit. The room has a thirty-foot-long boardroom table and full conference facilities. During the world cruise it is used as a private lounge for the exclusive use of those passengers who are booked for the full voyage. This part of the ship was originally the London Gallery, where works of art were on display and for sale. When the penthouses were installed it was converted to a quiet reading room and housed interesting pictures depicting old Cunard Line ships.

Astern of "D" stairway on each side are suites, once the site of the original kiosk-style shops. The *QE2* probably has the largest selection of shops at sea. A full range of clothing is available in both traditional and the latest fashions, in addition to jewelry, cameras, perfume, souvenirs, books, nautical antiques, and duty free liquor. Items indigenous to the countries the ship visits are also made available. The shopping arcade was moved to its present location in 1972, previously a lounge served by an island bar amidships. Windows on either side and at the after end look out over Boat Deck, and inboard, from the balcony, entertainment can be viewed in the Grand Lounge, one deck below. The interior design of the shops has changed periodically over the years, reflecting various trends. In 1987 more shops were added at the after end, and what was previously an open-air space known as the raised boat deck became known as the International Shopping Concourse. The area was further modified and extended and the name changed to the Royal Promenade.

Revolving doors on each side at the after end lead out onto the open deck; walking forward, you reach the steps leading up to the forward observation area (under the wings of the bridge).

The Boat Deck is popular with joggers and walkers — five circuits of the U-shaped track is one mile.

All the lifeboats are stowed in davits on the Boat Deck. There are twenty lifeboats of various types with a collective capacity for 2,346 people. In addition there are inflatable life rafts for a further 1,400 persons. Together, the life rafts and lifeboats provide a lifesaving capacity for 25 percent more persons than the ship is certified to carry. The six larger lifeboats have twin propellers, and are also used as tenders when the ship is at an anchorage port. The two forty-five-foot cruise tenders that were installed on the ship in December 1983 were especially designed for improving the service at anchorage ports. Although they carried 118 people, and their 212 horsepower engines gave a speed of 10 knots, they were not successful operationally and were removed in 1994. Replacement tender capacity was provided by converting two of the lifeboats to special purpose boats that can be used as tenders and lifeboats.

A large sculpture depicting "white horses" of the Atlantic Ocean provides the centerpiece of the Mauretania Restaurant. Passengers who dine in this restaurant have a choice of early or late seating for dinner.

The Crystal Bar, modeled after a similar design used on the *Queen Elizabeth*, provides a convenient meeting place for those dining in the Mauretania Restaurant and the Princess and Britannia Grills.

The Mauretania restaurant provides seating for 530 people. Many of the tables have spectacular ocean views.

The Theatre, with a capacity for 491 people on two levels, is the scene of a variety of events that include movies, plays, concerts, meetings, and lectures. (Photo courtesy of Simon Ranger.)

The Britannia Grill was added in 1990 and is very similar in character to the Princess Grill. It was renamed and redecorated in 1994 to commemorate Cunard Line's first ship, the paddle steamer *Britannia*. (Photo courtesy of Robin Ebers.)

The two new boats, numbers 13 and 14, have catamaran displacement hulls. They can each carry 112 people as a tender or 145 people as a lifeboat.

Upper Deck

A number of changes have taken place on this deck over the years. The first, in 1972, was the demise of the Lookout Bar, which was the only public room with a view looking forward over the bow. The space was converted to a kitchen to serve the Mauretania Restaurant. This restaurant was originally known as the Britannia Restaurant; escalators in the center led to the Colum-

The Golden Lion Pub, formerly known as the Theatre Bar, features live music and dancing and, being centrally located on Upper Deck, is a popular meeting place both day and night.

As well as a variety of slot machines, the Casino has tables for blackjack, craps, roulette, and poker.

bia kitchen, one deck below, which is where the waiters had to go to obtain food orders. Although the removal of the popular Lookout Bar was disappointing, taking out the escalators considerably improved the efficiency of service in the restaurant and increased the seating capacity to 792 persons.

Later the Britannia was divided into five different cultural-theme sections—Parisienne, Florentine, Londoner, Flamenco, and Oriental—and became known as the Tables of the World Restaurant. In 1977, it was changed again, to the Mauretania Restaurant, with the decor reverting to a central theme throughout. At the same time, the International Food Bazaar was introduced, as well as a dance floor under a mirrored ceiling. Further changes took place in 1994, when it was redecorated throughout. The dance floor was replaced by a bronze-colored aluminum sculpture by Althea Wynne depicting the "white horses" of the Atlantic Ocean. A model of the Caronia is displayed with her builder's plate at the after end of the restaurant. At the forward end there is a commissioned mural of the Caronia by Jane Human. The restaurant was renamed Caronia, but in April 1997 the names of the two main restaurants were reversed and it became the Mauretania once again. This restaurant seats 530 people.

Immediately aft of the Mauretania on the starboard side was the cocktail bar that served the Princess Grill Starboard Restaurant, which was installed when the ship was in Hamburg for refitting in 1990. In 1994 the whole area from one side of the ship to the other was reconstructed into the Crystal Bar. On the starboard side, stairs lead to the renamed Britannia Grill, one deck below. A new staircase was installed on the port side leading down to the Princess Grill.

The Grand Lounge has undergone a number of changes over the years. The most recent, in 1994, saw the removal of the double staircase on each side of the stage and the fitting of a movable carpet over the dance floor to increase the seating capacity when required.

One of the best alterations made in 1994 was the remodeling of the Yacht Club, which was extended out to the sides of the ship. For the first time, passengers could enjoy a view of the ocean from the bar.

Further astern on the starboard side is the entrance to the lower level of the theater/cinema, which has a capacity for 491 people. Gaby Schreiber, who was one of Britain's foremost female designers, was responsible for the theater. It is also used as a conference room, and a church when the captain holds an interdenominational service when the ship is at sea on a Sunday.

Next comes the Golden Lion Pub also on the starboard side themed with English pub-style furniture and bar. The pub was created in 1994, having previously been known as the Theatre Bar. When crossing to the port side at "D" stairway there is a showcase housing a selection of items from the Peter Radmore collection. Peter Radmore held one of the largest collections of Cunard memorabilia in the world until his death in 1992. Opposite are the silver plaques commemorating visits of members of the royal family. A more recent addition on display by the stairway is a silver cup presented to the R.M.S. *Laconia* on the occasion of the first Cunard Line world cruise in 1922.

Nearby is the cinema projection room and the control center for lighting and sound. Two large 70-millimeter projectors are used to show hundreds of films each year. On the world cruise alone enough films are carried to show a different one each day. Facilities also exist to show 16 and 35 millimeter films as well as video and audio slide presentations.

The Players Club Casino on the port side was totally remodeled during the Hamburg refitting in 1990 and was extended forward to include the area previously used as the Casino Hideaway Lounge. When the ship was first commissioned, most of this area was occupied by the Upper Deck library. This library, designed by Dennis Lennon, was over twice the size of the existing Quarter Deck library and was regarded by many as one of the most comfortable and peaceful rooms on the *QE2*. The port side entrance to the theater/cinema and the Crystal Bar is at the forward end of the casino.

The "E" stairway is amidships and has a bank of four elevators. These are the only lifts that stop at every floor between Boat Deck and Five Deck—eight stops in all. The three tapestries by Helen Barynina that hang on the landing commemorate the launching ceremony of the liner by Her Majesty Queen Elizabeth II on September 27, 1967.

Just across to starboard is an office shared by the cruise sales manager and the Cunard World Club host. The office and the adjacent band practice room combined were originally the Tour Office. Outboard on the starboard side is the gallery where photographers exhibit and sell pictures they have taken during the cruise.

Farther astern is the Grand Lounge. It was designed in its original form by Jon Bannenberg and was known as the Double Down Room. An impressive feature of the Double Down Room was a wide curved staircase at the after end connecting the room to the deck above. In 1987, when the room was remodeled, the curved staircase was removed and a twin staircase was fitted at the forward end with a retractable stage. The starlight paneled ceiling was fitted and a modern sound and lighting control box installed opposite the stage. Seating was arranged on three levels, which makes the room especially suited for the production shows and guest entertainers regularly featured on board. The 1994 refitting saw further changes to this room when the staircase was removed completely to increase the size. A spiral staircase to the Boat Deck was constructed farther aft outside the room. The Grand Lounge is one of the largest rooms in the ship, covering over 11,000 square feet. The room has seating for 538, which can be extended to 770 on special occasions.

Passing through the Grand Lounge on the port side is the cruise director's office, which replaced the travel and shore excursions center. The Tour and Travel office now replaces the Teen and Youth Club on the starboard side. This area was formerly the site of the flower shop, which has now been relocated on Three Deck aft. The Japanese armor display outside the office is one

Since the *QE2* began service she has always enjoyed a vast amount of open deck space compared to more modern passenger ships. Even more space was created when the Quarter Deck swimming pool was replaced by the Lido in 1994.

All the working surfaces and equipment in the kitchens are made of good-quality stainless steel. In addition to the captain's weekly inspection, regular visits are made by British and American health authorities to ensure that high standards of hygiene and food-handling practices are maintained. (Photo courtesy of Robin Ebers.)

Each of the ten giant cauldrons in the Columbia kitchen can be used to prepare 40 gallons of soup at a time. They are also used to boil fresh lobsters, which are a regular feature on the *QE2*'s extensive and varied menus. (Photo courtesy of Robin Ebers.)

Apart from fabric changes, the Princess Grill has maintained its original design since the Queen came into service in 1969. Many of the regular passengers choose their cabin category because they want to dine in this restaurant and its intimate atmosphere. Although situated on Quarter Deck, the Princess Grill can only be reached by a stairway down from the Crystal Bar or up from the Champagne Bar on One Deck. There is split-level seating for 102 guests.

of the most impressive of gifts presented to the ship since she commenced world cruises in 1975.

Outside the entrance to the Yacht Club is a large silver chalice presented to Samuel Cunard by the people of Boston in 1840. This, with large models of the *Britannia* and the *Asia*, paintings, and a bust of Samuel Cunard, gives an introduction to the early history of the line.

In 1987, the Yacht Club replaced the Double Down Bar; it can also be

The former Columbia Restaurant was extensively remodeled in 1994, and the name was changed to the Caronia Restaurant. It stretches the width of the ship and provides several tables on either side, each with and ocean view. (Photo courtesy of Kevin Boag.)

In the Chart Room, a display of navigational instruments and old maps complements the glass panel behind the bar showing the transatlantic routes taken by the *QE2*.

A piano that once graced the famous Cunard liner *Queen Mary* now takes pride of place in the seating area of the Chart Room Bar.

reached from the "G" stairway landing. The nautical decor with the wave-shaped ceiling features pictures and models of yachts that participated in the America's Cup races. In 1994 the popular glass-enclosed grand piano was removed and the internal width of the room extended to the sides of the ship. It was also extended farther aft to include the space previously used for the large passenger tenders.

Doors lead out to an open deck, which was added in 1994. The deck replaces the Magrodome, which was fitted over the Quarter Deck swimming pool in 1983. Steps lead aft, down to the Quarter Deck, or up to the Boat Deck.

Quarter Deck

The hatch lid of the cargo hold and the associated crane are on the Quarter Deck forward. Although not accessible to passengers, these can clearly be seen from the observation point on the Sports Deck. The crane can hold 5 tons and is used for loading provisions and stores. Vehicles used to be carried in the holds, but this is rarely the case now. The crane is a replacement and was fitted in 1987 at Bremerhaven. There used to be a portable swimming pool that fitted into the top level of the cargo hatch for the use of the crew when the ship was cruising. Toward the end of 1991, a new pool was made; it is lifted on to the port side of the hatch when required.

Astern of this area, the majority of the superstructure above the Quarter Deck level is made of aluminium separated from the steel below by a bi-metallic joint. This dual method of construction considerably reduced the weight of the ship and made it possible for her to have a draft much less than the old *Queen*s.

From the open deck, a door leads into the Caronia kitchen. The kitchen stretches the total width of the liner. A number of changes have taken place over the years that reflect the modernization of cooking appliances and improvements in hygiene and service efficiency. The Princess Grill is on the port side and is serviced by the Caronia kitchen. The grill, maintained in its original design and color scheme of Bordeaux red velvet and leather, creates an intimate and romantic atmosphere with seating for only 102 people. The life-size statues by Janine Janet representing the four elements—fire, earth, air, and water—are striking visible features made entirely of marine items such as shells, coral, and mother-of-pearl. Access to the Princess Grill is by the "C" elevator or a spiral stairway up from the Princess Grill Bar on One Deck or down from the Crystal Bar above.

On the opposite side of the ship is the Britannia Grill, with seating for 108 people. Previously named the Princess Grill Starboard, it is similar in size, atmosphere, and design to the original but with a different color scheme. Part of the decor includes a model of the *Britannia* and a print of a painting by John Stobbart that shows an incident during the winter of 1844 when she became

A large and elaborate model of the *Mauretania* (with a backdrop of the Atlantic Ocean created by Veronique Bour) graces Heritage Trail on the Quarter Deck.

The extension to the Library on Quarter Deck to incorporate a book shop in 1994 reflects the popularity of this room. The library is staffed by a full-time librarian and the book shop stocks a variety of publications and videos for sale.

trapped in ice in Boston. Space for this restaurant was partitioned off from the Caronia Restaurant during the 1986 refitting at Hamburg.

Adjoining the after end of the two grills is the Caronia Restaurant, which can accommodate 538 passengers. The captain hosts a table at the forward end in the center. He and the staff captain alternate tables every other evening in the Caronia and Mauretania restaurants. This restaurant was named the Columbia until 1994, when it was changed to the Mauretania. For operational reasons and by popular demand, the name was swapped in 1997 with that of the Caronia on the deck above.

As one leaves the Caronia by the center entrance, there is a large and spec-

The Queen's Room, a comfortable and spacious lounge spanning the width of the ship, is where afternoon tea is served and can be turned into a ballroom for formal dances or used for parties and special events. (Photo courtesy of Ocean Pictures)

The Lido Cafe provides an alternate dining place for all passengers. Breakfast, lunch, dinner, and midnight buffet are served here, and coffee is available around-the-clock. An air of informal elegance is created when the lights are dimmed in the evening.

The chef's artistic expertise is demonstrated at the Gala Midnight Buffet with a giant ice carving of a sea monster as the centerpiece. (Photo courtesy of Simon Ranger.)

tacular model of the *Mauretania*. Veronique Bour was commissioned to create the backdrop to the model depicting the Atlantic Ocean.

To the starboard side is what could probably be the largest oil on canvas afloat. Painted by Tom Hemy in 1908, it measures 99 by 73 inches and depicts the *Mauretania* leaving the Tyne on her maiden voyage.

The Chart Room Bar is a few feet away. This was formerly the Midships Bar and was substantially remodeled during the 1994 refitting. The calligraphic frieze was created by Brody Neuenschwander. It is complemented by a display of old navigational instruments, including a brass armillary sphere (showing the relationship of planets to the earth and the signs of the zodiac), which was presented to Cunard by the Institute of London Underwriters when the ship was commissioned. The previous decor of dark green and gold leaf (on the ceiling) had remained the same since the ship was launched, and although it no longer exists, it was a credit to the designers, Dennis Lennon and Partners.

On the opposite side of the ship is the Book Shop, created in 1994 in place of the Card Room. The Book Shop is a very popular room on the ship, particularly when authors are on board and their books are made available for purchase and signing. Adjacent to the shop is the library, originally designed by Michael Inchbald. In addition to the continuously updated selection of newspapers, magazines, current best sellers, classics, novels, and reference books, there is a wide selection of foreign language publications and books in large print. Two computers with a CD-ROM reference library are also available for passengers to browse at their leisure. The oil painting of the *Cuba* by Samuel Walters, in the library, is one of the finest marine paintings owned by Cunard.

Spanning the width of the ship, the Queen's Room has a warm, inviting atmosphere day or night. It is the scene of many activities, from yoga classes in the morning, afternoon tea, and pre-dinner cocktail parties to the evening cabaret. The structural columns are encased in great inverted trumpets of white fiberglass. The trumpet shape in reverse used to be reflected in the design of white chairs upholstered in natural hide, but these were replaced by cubelike armchairs in brown leather prior to the more classic style that the room has now been furnished in. At the forward end there is a bronze bust of Her Royal Highness Queen Elizabeth II by Oscar Nemon elegantly recessed into the bulkhead. At the after end on each side of the stage are three framed royal standards reflecting the strong connection that exists between the Cunard Line and the royal family.

Colorful murals commissioned from the artist Giancarlo Impiglia adorn the walls in the passageways leading from the Queen's Room to the entrance to the Lido. On the port side you first pass the teen center, called Club 2000, complete with the latest video game machines.

The creation of the Lido as an alternative dining area and the removal of the swimming pool were among the major changes made in 1994. The center of the area incorporates the main food preparation unit and two buffets allow service to passengers from separate lines from either side. There is a separate dessert buffet station as well as a bar and 24-hour coffee facilities. Food is served here at all the regular mealtimes, and there is an artistic midnight buffet. David Hicks designed the original room, then known as the Q4.

The first stage of major changes made to the Q4 came during the period it took the government to restore the ship to service after the 1982 Falkland Campaign. The bar was removed from the after end and temporarily located on the port side. This enabled the after end to be opened up, creating a much

The small, intimate Champagne Bar is on the port side of One Deck. There is direct access to the Princess Grill by a spiral stairway or an elevator. (Photo courtesy of Simon Ranger.)

lighter and therefore more versatile room in the daytime. A small kitchen provides the facilities for breakfast and lunch buffets.

The second stage was carried out in 1983 in Bremerhaven. The bar was repositioned and the glass floor laid with the adjacent bandstand and control center for music and lighting. The prefabricated Magradome was lifted into position over the swimming pool within two days of the vessel's arrival at Bremerhaven. The retractable glass roof created a complete indoor/outdoor entertainment and leisure area.

One Deck

One Deck is the longest deck on the ship, having a total length from stem to stern of 963 feet. The forward part is known as the foredeck and it can be seen from the observation point on the Sports Deck under the bridge. When the ship is docking, an officer will be seen right forward supervising the mooring operations, which take place from the deck below.

There are two anchors housed in the bow, each weighing $12 \frac{1}{2}$ tons. The anchor chain, or cable, as it is known to the seafarer, leads from the anchor up the hawse pipe and along the deck, passing around the capstan and then down into the chain locker. The total length of each chain is 1,080 feet; the links are 4 inches in diameter and have a breaking strain of just over 500 tons. A spare anchor used to be kept on the port side of the foredeck. It was previously housed in the stem but was repositioned following damage during a North Atlantic storm in 1981. During an earlier storm, in 1976, the spare anchor was lost altogether and now lies on the ocean floor somewhere mid-Atlantic. In 1995, the starboard anchor was damaged and had to be replaced so at the same time it was decided to keep the spare anchor ashore. Between the an-

The cabins on Four and Five Decks are arranged to make them as efficient as possible. Some of the cabins are fitted with an alternative third upper-bunk, which can be folded away when not needed.

chors the forward whistle can be seen mounted on a tripod. It is operated by remote control from the bridge. If the ship is in fog or there is restricted visibility it can be programmed to sound automatically at one- or two-minute intervals.

Aft and inboard are staff quarters. There is a shop, a hairdresser, a gymnasium, a library, recreation rooms, and a mess room with its own servery and galley. The crew have their own computer learning center, which is administrated by the crew personnel manager, whose office is nearby.

Just astern and in the passenger area is the photographers' dark room. The team of four resident photographers can produce around 1,600 pictures a day in addition to making video films of the cruise.

Near "C" stairway on the port side is the Champagne Bar. The Princess Grill Restaurant, one deck above, can be reached from the small and intimate bar by the spiral stairway that is a feature of the room.

On One Deck by the "D" stairway is the Cunard Collection Shop, where a variety of logo items and clothing are sold. Prior to this, it was the Harrod's of London shop. Installed in 1984, it was the only branch of Harrod's at sea. When the ship was commissioned, this was the One Deck Shop and sold exclusive jewelry. During the 1972 conversion the shop was moved up to the Boat Deck, and the area was converted into a bar, known as the Club Atlantic. When the liner *France* ended her service on the North Atlantic run, staff members from the ship were employed on board the *QE2* to work in the bar. The bar was subsequently closed, and the area converted to a shop specializing in china and crystal. In the foyer of the "D" stairway there is an embossed leather picture depicting old sailing ships. This picture was originally hung in the first-class smoke room of the German steamer Kaiser Wilhelm der Grosse. At the time of her commissioning in 1898, the vessel was the world's largest passenger ship and was the first to gain the Blue Riband for Germany. The

The outside swimming pool, filled with seawater, is the scene of King Neptune's visit on the annual world cruise. The pool is conveniently located next to the Pavilion Cafe, and changing rooms with showers are provided nearby.

A resident instructor is in regular attendance at the Computer Learning Centre to provide tuition at all levels. Since this photograph was taken, all the computers have been replaced by Micron equipment to enable passengers to send their own e-mail.

The Midships Lobby on Two Deck is where most passengers see the interior of the ship for the first time. The walls of the Lobby feature murals depicting the history of Cunard Line since the company was founded by Sir Samuel Cunard in 1839.

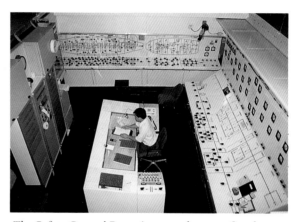

The Safety Control Room is manned twenty-four hours a day. A vast amount of information about the safety features of the ship is displayed on the array of consoles, and there are direct communication links to the bridge and engine room.

picture was presented to the *QE2* by the Lloyd Werft shipyard, which carried out the re-engining and major conversions of 1986–1987.

Before the installation of the penthouses, the cabins on One Deck were the highest-grade accommodations available on the ship. Many have connecting doors to adjoining cabins. Over 70 percent of the cabins on the *QE2* are outboard, and all rooms have their own bath and/or shower. The majority of the bathrooms were totally refurbished in 1994. Each cabin has a console for selecting music or radio news broadcasts from a selection of six channels. As a

The unique Midships Suite is situated on Two Deck near the D stairway. This spacious stateroom was created in 1990 from former office space and staff accommodation and has been in popular demand ever since. In 1998, it was occupied by President Nelson Mandela and Mrs. Graça Machel when they traveled on the ship between Durban and Capetown.

safety feature, priority announcements from the bridge are heard in all cabins regardless of whether the channels are switched on or off. A telephone is connected to a central exchange from which calls can be made to anywhere in the world. The telephone system was completely renewed in 1987 to provide automatic wake-up calls and direct dialing throughout the ship and ship-to-shore worldwide. Cabins were also fitted with televisions.

Toward the after end of One Deck, by the "G" stairway, is the hair and beauty salon, operated by Steiner's of London. Here, highly qualified hair stylists cater to men and women. The salon is constructed on the open plan principle so that shampoo, setting, and drying areas are located in the main body of the room with adjoining private sections for beauty care consultation.

Passing the salon, doors lead to the Pavilion, which was installed in 1994. It features a food service area for breakfast and lunch, a bar, and changing rooms. The swimming pool was totally refurbished in 1987, with the addition of jacuzzies and the Cunard lion depicted in vivid red mosaic tiles.

Two Deck

In the foremost part of the vessel on Two Deck are the mooring winches. When the *QE2* is in port, she will normally be made fast to the quay by three synthetic fiber ropes and three or four flexible steel wire ropes at each end of the ship. The ropes are set in position first, followed by the wires. The wires have a breaking strain of 103 tons and are attached to self-tensioning winches, which keep them tight irrespective of tidal conditions. Also in this area are the bosun's stores and paint lockers, where enough stock is carried to enable maintenance to be carried out.

The Purser's Office on Two Deck can be compared to the reception desk of a large hotel, and it is where all day-to-day inquiries are dealt with. A full range of banking services is provided by the Bureau de Change on the opposite side of the square. (Photo courtesy of Robin Ebers.)

QE2's TV studio and control center is one of the most sophisticated networks of its kind afloat. It produces a continuous variety of programs for the multichannel televisions fitted in every passenger cabin. Live interviews can be broadcast direct to each cabin from the studio.

The Computer Learning Centre is situated in the square near "A" stairway. This facility is equipped with sixteen computers, and a resident instructor is available to give courses on their use. Nearby there is a large carved wooden plaque presented by the First Sea Lord, Sir John Fieldhouse, to commemorate the Falkland Campaign. The baggage master has an office and storerooms just before the midships lobby on the port side. The baggage master will often be seen moving baggage around while the ship is at sea, especially on the word cruise. It is not uncommon for passengers to have a dozen or so trunks that hold clothes that will be worn once and then packed away again.

The midships lobby on Two Deck is where most passengers and visitors first come on board. The gangway can be placed on either the port or the starboard side of the ship. This circular sunken area with banquette seating makes an ideal meeting place. The decor was changed in 1994 to incorporate mural panels by the British artist Peter Sutton to illustrate various heritage elements of Cunard and the *QE2* on the curved bulkheads. The large brass ship's bell is at the after end of the lobby. It has traditionally been used for christening babies and for ringing out the old year and ringing in the new.

Centrally placed within the ship, the Safety Control Room (SCR) is, like the bridge and the engine room, manned 24 hours a day at sea and in port. Master plans of the ship showing all the safety features are on display.

The ship is divided into compartments, each of which can be made completely watertight by hydraulic doors remotely controlled from the bridge. Indicators set out in a diagram on the bridge and in the SCR show whether the doors are in the open or closed position.

The ship is also divided into eight zones with fire-resistant bulkheads and doors that can be remotely closed from the Safety Control Room to prevent fire from spreading. All the cabins and public rooms on the *QE2* have automatic sprinklers. Should one of these be set off, an audible alarm is triggered on the bridge and in the SCR, and a visual indicator of the danger area will appear on the master diagrams. The break-glass alarm push buttons situated throughout the ship are similarly indicated. To comply with recent safety legislation, all cabins, lockers, office space, and public areas around the ship have been fitted with smoke detectors, which set off alarms in the SCR and on the bridge if any detection is made. In addition, crew specially trained in shipboard fire-fighting techniques patrol the ship at regular intervals to

The daily program is packed with a choice of activities provided for all moods and tastes. The program is delivered to every cabin, and it is one of the many items produced each day by the four printers employed on board. (Photo courtesy of Robin Ebers.)

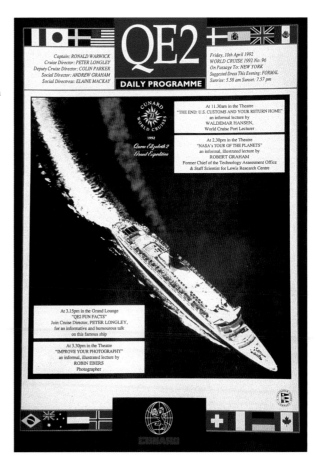

Three Deck, with 186 cabins, is the longest passenger deck on the ship. This picture of the corridor gives an impressive indication of the length of the vessel. (Photo courtesy of Robin Ebers.)

supplement the detecting aids. Every crew member joining the ship is required to undergo a *QE2* safety familiarization course, and the certificate obtained upon completion must be revalidated every two years.

Consoles in the Safety Control Room also indicate the amount of fuel, fresh water, and ballast water contained in all the tanks. Depending on speed, fuel may be consumed at a varying rate up to eighteen tons per hour, so it is necessary to adjust the water-ballast tanks constantly. The control of all pumping and transfer of water ballast and fuel is carried out from the control room. Accumulation of water in the bilges is sensed by electrically operated probes and indicated on another console where valves and pumps can be operated directly from the control room.

The purser's office, on Two Deck, by the "F" stairway, is the scene of many passenger-related activities and can be compared with the reception desk at a large hotel. The staff on duty at the front desk deal with the majority of passenger inquiries or channel them in the proper direction. A department within the office handles all passport, visa, and immigration matters. On the opposite side of the square is a branch of the Travelex Bank, which offers a full range of banking and financial services, including foreign currency conversions, check cashing, and the transferring of funds. All major credit cards are accepted. Passenger accounts are dealt with at the cashier's section of the purser's office, approached from the square at the "G" stairway. The safe deposit box facility, situated on the "G" stairway square nearby, is administered by the purser's department.

The doctor's consultation room and waiting lounge are located on the port side of "G" square. A doctor is in attendance at regularly posted hours during the day. No appointment is necessary.

At the extreme after end of Two Deck are mooring arrangements similar to those at the forward end of the vessel.

Three Deck

An impressive indication of the length and structure of the ship can be seen on Three Deck. Looking aft from the forward end, the deck head appears to come into contact with the deck due to the curvature built into the construction of the ship. The synagogue, designed by Professor Misha Black, is located by the "A" stairway. The room is peacefully decorated in blue with ash panels.

Further aft there is a TV studio and control center for all the cabin entertainment. Feature films, documentaries, and news bulletins are shown continuously on selected channels. One channel is dedicated to navigational information directly linked to the satellite position-finding system on the bridge. Another channel is coupled to a television camera mounted on the top of the bridge. The studio was the site of the old telephone exchange. Staff used to be on duty at the exchange day and night, as all calls made from passenger

The majority of the cabins on *QE2* have a window or porthole looking out over the sea. This picture was taken from a crew cabin on Six Deck. Being near the waterline, the porthole has a heavy steel deadlight that can be securely closed in very bad weather. (Photo courtesy of Robin Ebers.)

cabin telephones had to be manually connected by the operators. This was all replaced by the computer-supported automated system installed in 1987.

At the after end of Three Deck, on the starboard side, is a laundromat and ironing area for passengers' personal use. Adjacent is the flower shop, where all the foliage arrangements for the ship are prepared.

Four Deck

Four Deck is almost entirely passenger cabins, with crew quarters at the extreme ends fore and aft. Gangways are sometimes located on Four Deck, and facilities exist for cars to be taken on through the same entrances.

Five Deck

As on Four Deck, there are crew accommodations at the extreme ends of Five Deck with passenger cabins in between.

Along each side of the ship there are nine shell doors. These doors form part of the hull. When closed, they are secured by steel bolts and are watertight. The doors have various uses, such as for gangways and for loading and unloading stores and cars. When the ship is at anchor, pontoons are lowered from the Boat Deck and are made fast by the opening in use, which provides

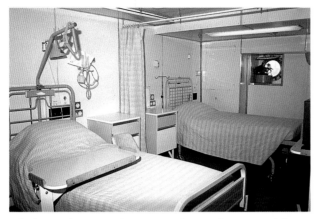

The hospital is situated on Six Deck near the center of the ship where the motion is less evident. Care is provided by highly qualified medical staff consisting of two doctors and three nurses who are all permanently employed by Cunard Line. (Photo courtesy of Robin Ebers.)

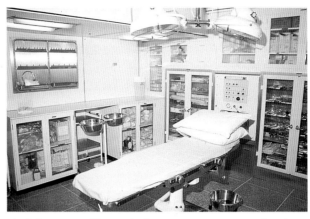

The fully equipped hospital is kept in a constant state of readiness to deal with medical emergencies at sea. The sealed lockers behind the operating table contain sterilized instruments available for immediate use. (Photo courtesy of Robin Ebers.)

The *QE2* Spa is one of the finest of its kind afloat. Among the features included are the steam rooms, hydrotherapy baths, massage rooms, and high pressure water massage. (Photo courtesy of Robin Ebers.)

Next to the heated swimming pool on Seven Deck, certified instructors are in attendance to offer exercise classes at the Fitness Center.

boarding platforms for the ship's launches. Amidships on each side, the doors give access to the bunkering stations. Oil can be bunkered at a rate of 600 tons per hour on each side. Water can also be taken aboard at these same locations.

Watertight doors are fitted at regular intervals along each side of Five Deck and below. The doors divide the ship into fifteen separate watertight compartments and are tested every day the ship is at sea by remote control from the bridge. These doors can also be closed or opened by controls alongside each individual door or from Four Deck.

Six Deck

Six Deck is very much a working area of the ship, and the passageway that runs forward to aft on the starboard side is known as the "working alleyway." Crew quarters stretch from the forward end down the port side to the after end. Near the forward end is an administrative office, which deals with the day-to-day affairs of crew members.

The Printer's Shop is also down here. A variety of items are produced, including menus, daily programs, newspapers, special invitations, and all the general stationery requirements of the ship.

The hospital is located by the "C" stairway on Six Deck. Being near the waterline and at the center of the ship, it is free from the movement that is

The laundry and dry-cleaning service is operated by very dedicated members of the staff who work night and day to provide fresh linen and a personal service for over 2,500 passengers and crew. (Photo courtesy of Robin Ebers.)

Drive-on drive-off ramps are available in Southampton, Cherbourg, and New York for passengers who wish to transport their cars across the Atlantic Ocean. The elevator, on the left in this picture, is mounted on a turntable to facilitate the stowage and removal of the vehicles. (Photo courtesy of Robin Ebers.)

sometimes evident on the upper decks of the vessel. Its location adjacent to working areas also makes it easily accessible to the crew. The hospital has five wards, each with two beds. Serving the wards is a duty room, where indicators show if a patient requires attention. There is an oxygen and nitrous oxide storage room from which direct lines of each gas lead to every bed in the wards, operating room, and dentist's office. A well-stocked pharmacy caters to a wide variety of medical complaints. To assist with diagnoses there is a small laboratory where pathological tests can be carried out. Should surgery be required, there is a fully equipped operating room. Basic operating instrument packs are kept ready and are sterilized at regular intervals. Specialized instruments can be quickly sterilized in the autoclave.

Separate, but enclosed within the hospital area, are a physiotherapy ward, a lead-lined X-ray room, the fully equipped dentist's office, and a mortuary.

The hospital is manned by two doctors, three nurses, and three medical attendants. During the annual world cruise this team is sometimes supplemented with a fourth nurse, a physiotherapist, and a dentist. Clinics are held twice daily for both the passengers and the crew. Should an unexpected emergency occur outside clinic hours, the whole medical team can be called by a special alert procedure to attend a patient wherever his or her location. The team and accompanying emergency equipment can be assembled within a very few minutes.

Moving toward midships, there are the electrical and plumbers' workshops and the technical offices by the entrance to the engine room.

Aft of the engine room is the Health Spa. Access is from Five Deck via the "F" stairway or elevator. The spa, the first ever at sea, was introduced in 1982 and was directed by the Golden Door of Encino, California. In 1992 it was modernized and remodeled by Steiner's of London. A total fitness and exercise program is run by Steiner personnel to fulfill the needs of individual passengers. Daily activities include yoga, aerobic exercise, jogging, swimming, and lectures on nutrition, stress management, and a variety of other topics relating to health. The spa has a large exercise area, a pool with a teak platform for hydrocalisthenics, and three large jacuzzi whirlpool baths. The latter facilities replace the Turkish baths.

Seven and Eight Decks

Right forward on seven and eight decks is a bulk beer store capable of holding a total of 13,000 gallons in 27 stainless steel tanks. The tanks are in an air-conditioned room; beer used to be piped directly to the bars. This equipment has not been used for several years.

The domestic storerooms are all situated forward in the ship and provide a total capacity of about 20,000 cubic feet of storage. Additional space is gained by using the holds when the ship is on the annual world cruise. Number two hold is used exclusively for the storage of wines and liquor. The retail value of the stock of liquor alone at the start of the world cruise is in excess of $2 million. Over 20,000 bottles of wine are carried, varying in price from $12.00 to $560 a bottle.

The laundry stretches the full width of the ship and is equipped with machines capable of washing and pressing the restaurant, bed, and bath linens used daily by the passengers and crew. The dry-cleaning department provides a full valet service.

Cars driven on board at Four or Five Deck levels are taken below to the holds by the two car lifts. The lifts are of the turret type, so they can turn, thus enabling the cars to be driven off into the holds in any direction. When the *QE2* was first commissioned in 1969 about 70 cars could be carried, but the space has gradually been taken up in order to carry essential stores and spare parts, and now there is room for only twelve vehicles. In 1987, number six hold was converted into a garbage processing plant. Garbage from throughout the ship is delivered to this area, where it is sorted, shredded, compacted, and stowed in a refrigerated storeroom. It remains there until it can be landed ashore. This facility replaces the incinerator equipment that was situated on Six Deck.

On Seven Deck, reached by "C" stairway or via the elevator, is the second indoor swimming pool, saunas, and a gymnasium.

The entrance to the Engine Control Room is on Seven Deck. From here there is access to the various engine compartments and machinery described in Chapter Eight.

Builders: Upper Clyde Shipbuilders
Keel laid: July 5, 1965
Launched: September 20, 1967
Maiden voyage: May 2, 1969
Port of registry: Southampton
Signal letters: GBTT
Official number: 336703

Tonnage
Gross tonnage: 70,327
Net tonnage: 37,182

Dimensions
Length overall: 963' 00" (293.52m)
Breadth overall: 105' 2½" (32.07m)
Bridge height of eye: 95' 00" (28.96m)
Bridge to stem: 238' 2" (72.59m)
Bridge to stern: 724' 10" (220.93m)
Mast height above keel: 200' 1½"
   (61.00m)
Funnel height above keel: 204' ½"
   (62.22m)

Draft
Loaded draft: 32' 7_" (9,994mm)
Freeboard: 23' 6_" (7,169mm)
FWA: 7½" (190mm)
TPI/cm: 151.5 (60.6)

Tanks
Fresh water: 1,850 tons
Laundry water: 532 tons
Boiler feed water: 113 tons
Ballast: 4,610 tons

Fuel oil: 4,311 tons
Lubricating oil: 383 tons
Diesel oil: 231 tons
Oily water: 243 tons
Sewage: 269 tons
Sludge: 13 tons

Anchors
Forward: 2 at 12½ tons, each attached
   to a 4"-diameter cable of 12 shackles
   in length equal to 1,080 feet
Aft: 1 at 7 ¼ tons attached to a
   3"-diameter cable of 8 shackles in
   length equal to 720 feet

Machinery
9 Diesel engines
Makers: MAN-B&W of West Germany
Type: 9L 58/64
Nine-cylinder medium speed
Weight: 220 tons
Capacity: 10,625kW at 400 rpm

9 Alternators
Makers: GEC Turbine Generators,
   Ltd., England
Rated: 10,500kW at 400 rev/min
Output: 10kV at a frequency of 60Hz

2 Propulsion motors
Makers: GEC Large Machines Ltd.,
   England
Rated: 44MW synchronous running
   at 144 rev/min.

Weight: 300 tons

2 Propellers
Makers: Lips BV., Holland
Diameter: 19 feet
Weight: 42 tons
Type: Variable-pitch outward turning

2 Bow thrusters
Makers: Stone Kamewa
Power: 1,000 hp each
Type: Variable-pitch propeller

4 Stabilizers
Makers: Brown Brothers
Length: 12 feet
Area: 70 square feet each

Steering gear
Makers: Brown Brothers
Type: 4 ram electrohydraulic

Rudder
Makers: A/S Strommens Vaerksted,
   Norway
Weight: 75 tons

Passenger and Safety Certification
Passengers: 1,952
Crew: 1,015
Total: 2,967

Lifeboats: 20; total capacity: 2,346
   persons
Life rafts: 56; total capacity: 1,400
   persons
Buoyant apparatus: 5; total capacity:
   100 persons
Lifejackets: 3,116 adult
   200 children
Lifebuoys: 30

July 25, 1974	Aadalsnes, Norway
Mar. 22, 1975	Acapulco, Mexico
Feb. 19, 1985	Adelaide, Australia
Dec. 10, 1991	Agadir, Morocco
Oct. 1, 1983	Ajaccio, Corsica
May 28, 1981	Alesund, Norway
Apr. 7, 1976	Alexandria, Egypt
Sept. 24, 1997	Algeciras, Spain
May 30, 1997	Alghero, Sardinia
Oct. 12, 1994	Alicante, Spain
Feb. 10, 1996	Ambon, Indonesia
Dec. 13, 1995	Amsterdam, Holland
Feb. 18, 1995	Apra, Guam
Mar. 27, 1995	Aquaba, Jordan
Apr. 16, 1982	Arrecife, Lanzarote
May 20, 1982	Ascension Island, South Atlantic
Apr. 21, 1973	Ashdod, Israel
Feb. 14, 1978	Auckland, New Zealand
Mar. 24, 1978	Balboa, Panama
Feb. 22, 1975	Bali, Indonesia
May 5, 1985	Baltimore, United States of America
July 23, 1981	Bar Harbor, United States of America
Apr. 29, 1974	Barcelona, Spain
Dec. 13, 1982	Basseterre, St. Kitts
Feb. 13, 1978	Bay of Islands, New Zealand
July 29, 1973	Bergen, Norway
Aug. 26, 1983	Block Island, United States of America
Feb. 11, 1975	Bombay, India

Oct. 1, 1971	Boston, United States of America
May 9, 1975	Bremerhaven, Germany
June 21, 1993	Brest, France
Nov. 22, 1969	Bridgetow, Barbados
Feb. 24, 1983	Brisbane, Australia
Oct. 20, 1989	Cadiz, Spain
Oct. 15, 1991	Cagiliari, Sardinia
Jan. 25, 1986	Callao, Peru
May 20, 1998	Canakkale, Turkey
Apr. 30, 1974	Cannes, France
Oct. 11, 1973	Canso Strait, Nova Scotia
Nov. 10, 1970	Cape Town, South Africa
Dec. 3, 1969	Caracas Bay, Curacao
Mar. 26, 1975	Cartagena, Colombia
Dec. 17, 1970	Castries, St. Lucia
Dec. 3, 1989	Charleston, United
Nov. 25, 1969	Charlotte Amalie, St. Thomas
Nov. 15, 1969	Cherbourg, France
May 27, 1969	Cóbh, Republic of Ireland
Feb. 17, 1975	Colombo, Sri Lanka
Oct. 9, 1973	Come by Chance, Newfoundland
Mar. 17, 1980	Constantza, Romania
Feb. 13, 1996	Cooktown, Australia
July 19, 1972	Copenhagen, Denmark
May 24, 1997	Corfu, Greece
Aug. 12, 1983	Cornerbrook, Newfoundland

Jan. 19, 1986   Cozumel, Mexico
Mar. 25, 1975   Cristobal, Panama
Mar. 10, 1979   Dairen, China
Oct. 30, 1970   Dakar, Senegal
Mar. 4, 1995   Danang, Vietnam
Mar. 5, 1993   Darwin, Australia
Mar. 5, 1980   Djibouti, Republic of Djibouti
Mar. 22, 1997   Dubai, United Arab Emirates
July 14, 1997   Dun Laoghaire, Ireland
Nov. 7, 1970   Durban, South Africa
Feb. 20, 1989   Ensenada, Mexico
Sept. 6, 1982   Falmouth, England
July 3, 1981   Flaam, Norway
Nov. 24, 1969   Fort de France, Martinique
Feb. 10, 1971   Frederiksted, St. Croix
Feb. 1, 1971   Freeport, Bahamas
May 18, 1982   Freetown, Sierra Leone
Feb. 22, 1985   Fremantle, Australia
Apr. 2, 1970   Funchal, Madeira
July 28, 1973   Geiranger, Norway
May 21, 1983   Genoa, Italy
Apr. 24, 1970   Gibraltar, Crown Colony
July 25, 1990   Greenock, Scotland
May 27, 1982   Grytviken, South Georgia
Apr. 24, 1973   Haifa, Israel
Oct. 11, 1973   Halifax, Nova Scotia
July 21, 1972   Hamburg, Germany
Mar. 25, 1971   Hamilton, Bermuda
July 25, 1973   Hammerfest, Norway
July 28, 1973   Hellesylt, Norway
Aug. 1, 1996   Helsinki, Finland
Jan. 22, 1997   Hilo, Hawaiian Islands
Feb. 20, 1978   Hobart, Tasmania
Feb. 27, 1975   Hong Kong, Crown Colony
Mar. 15, 1975   Honolulu, Hawaiian Islands
Sept. 29, 1983   Ibiza, Balearic Islands
Aug. 17, 1984   Ingonish, Nova Scotia

Sept. 4, 1995   Invergordon, Scotland
Apr. 29, 1970   Istanbul, Turkey
Mar. 13, 1979   Kagoshima, Japan
Mar. 29, 1983   Kailua Kona, Hawaiian Islands
Feb. 2, 1990   Kaohsiung, Taiwan
Mar. 1, 1986   Karachi, Pakistan
Feb. 15, 1984   Keelung, Taiwan
Jan. 8, 1970   Kingston, Jamaica
Jan. 24, 1971   Kingstown, St. Vincent
Aug. 1, 1998   Kirkwall, Orkney Islands
Mar. 5, 1975   Kobe, Japan
Mar. 1, 1977   Kota Kinabalu, Malaysia
Dec. 25, 1981   Kralendijk, Bonaire
Apr. 2, 1995   Kusadasi, Turkey
Apr. 30, 1984   La Coruna, Spain
Jan. 11, 1971   La Guaira, Venezuela
Oct. 28, 1996   La Rochelle, France
Feb. 14, 1991   Lae, Papua New Guinea
Mar. 4, 1992   Laem Chabang, Thailand
Mar. 20, 1982   Lahaina, Hawaiian Islands
Dec. 28, 1968   Las Palmas, Grand Canary Island
Feb. 2, 1998   Lautoka, Fiji
May 2, 1969   Le Havre, France
June 13, 1993   Leith, England
Apr. 28, 1969   Lisbon, Portugal
July 24, 1990   Liverpool, England
May 24, 1998   Livorno, Italy
Sept. 25, 1991   Long Island Sound, United States of America
July 20, 1997   Longyerbyen, Spitzbergen
Mar. 19, 1975   Los Angeles, United States of America
Nov. 3, 1970   Luanda, Angola
Feb. 11, 1985   Lyttelton, New Zealand
Feb. 18, 1982   Madras, India
Feb. 2, 1986   Magellan Straits, Chile
Feb. 8, 1975   Mahe, Seychelles

Oct. 12, 1982	Malaga, Spain	Feb. 28, 1982	Pattaya, Thailand
Mar. 20, 1998	Male, Maldives	Mar. 1, 1984	Penang, Malaysia
Mar. 11, 1978	Manila, Phillipines	Apr. 25, 1982	Philadelphia, United States of America
Oct. 30, 1990	Marseilles, France		
June 4, 1985	Martha's Vineyard, United States of America	Nov. 17, 1971	Phillipsburg, St. Maarten
		Apr. 27, 1970	Piraeus, Greece
Mar. 1, 1990	Masan, South Korea	Nov. 17, 1995	Playa Blanca, Lanzarotte
Apr. 4, 1978	Mazatlan, Mexico		
Feb. 22, 1978	Melbourne, Australia	Aug. 8, 1995	Plymouth, England
June 6, 1973	Messina, Sicily	Dec. 27, 1985	Pointe-a-Pitre, Guadeloupe
Nov. 15, 1997	Miami, United States of America	Oct. 22, 1997	Ponta Delgada, Azores
Feb. 18, 1978	Milford Sound, New Zealand	Dec. 30, 1970	Port au Prince, Haiti
Feb. 5, 1975	Mombasa, Kenya	Dec. 8, 1980	Port Canaveral, United States of America
Apr. 4, 1992	Monte Carlo, Monaco		
Feb. 4, 1979	Montevideo, Uruguay		
Feb. 9, 1983	Moorea, Tahiti	Feb. 4, 1992	Port Chalmers, New Zealand
Mar. 23, 1997	Muscat, Oman		
Jan. 9, 1971	Mustique, Grenadine Islands	Dec. 21, 1971	Port Everglades, United States of America
Mar. 10, 1977	Nagasaki, Japan		
May 2, 1970	Naples, Italy	Feb. 23, 1982	Port Kelang, Malaysia
Mar. 10, 1971	Nassau, Bahamas	Feb. 12, 1982	Port Louis, Mauritius
May 7, 1969	New York, United States of America	Mar. 1, 1978	Port Moresby, Papua New Guinea
June 11, 1988	Newhaven, United States of America	Dec. 29, 1969	Port of Spain, Trinidad
Oct. 2, 1982	Newport, United States of America	Mar. 20, 1981	Port Said, Egypt
		Jan. 22, 1993	Port Stanley, Falkland Islands
Nov. 13, 1985	Newport News, United States of America		
		Dec. 5, 1988	Porto Grande, Cape Verde Island
Jan. 15, 1972	Norfolk, United States of America	Oct. 16, 1984	Praia da Rocha, Portugal
Feb. 11, 1981	Nuku'alofa, Tonga Islands	Feb. 2, 1993	Puerto Caldera, Costa Rica
Aug. 2, 1996	Nynashamn, Sweden	Jan. 21, 1986	Puerto Limon, Costa Rica
Apr. 12, 1976	Odessa, Russia		
Feb. 8, 1971	Oranjestad, Aruba	Jan. 31, 1986	Puerto Montt, Chile
Apr. 2, 1988	Osaka, Japan	Feb. 17, 1989	Puerto Vallarta, Mexico
July 18, 1972	Oslo, Norway		
Jan. 30, 1995	Pago Pago, American Samoa	Mar. 10, 1982	Pusan, South Korea
		Mar. 19, 1983	Qingdao, China
Oct. 3, 1983	Palermo, Sicily	July 20, 1981	Quebec, Canada
Apr. 30, 1972	Palma de Mallorca, Balearic Islands	July 17, 1995	Queensferry, Scotland
		Feb. 11, 1983	Rarotonga, Cook Islands
Mar. 25, 1975	Panama Canal Transit		
Feb. 5, 1978	Papeete, Tahiti	July 8, 1996	Reykjavik, Iceland

Captains who have sailed in command of the *QE2* and the date of their first appointment as such:

Commodore W. E. Warwick, C.B.E., R.D., R.N.R., Dec. 23, 1968

Captain G. E. Smith,* June 12, 1969

Captain F. J. Storey,* R.D., R.N.R., Oct. 17, 1969

Captain J. E. Wolfenden,* R.D., R.N.R., May 8, 1970

Captain W. J. Law, R.D., R.N.R., June 19, 1970

Captain M. Hehir, June 3, 1971

Captain P. Jackson, Aug. 6, 1973

Captain R. H. Arnott, R.D., R.N.R., May 22, 1976

Captain L. R. W. Portet, R.D., Cdr. R.N.R., Apr. 13, 1977

Commodore T. D. Ridley,* R.D., Capt. R.N.R., Aug. 26, 1978

Captain A. J. Hutcheson,* R.D., R.N.R., Mar. 13, 1982

Captain R. Wadsworth,* May 15, 1983

Captain K. H. Stanley,* Apr. 9, 1984

Captain A. C. Bennell, R.D., R.N.R., July 10, 1987

Captain R. A. Woodall, R.D., R.N.R., Nov. 1, 1987

Commodore J. Burton-Hall, R.D., Cdr. R.N.R., Mar. 7, 1990

Captain R. W. Warwick, Lt. Cdr. R.N.R., F.N.I., July 26, 1990

Captain L. R. Hasell, Apr. 12, 1997

*Denotes captains who sailed as a relief to the permanent captain on one or more voyages.

Appendix 4: The Crew of the Queen Elizabeth 2

Depending on the nature of the voyage and the number of passengers carried, there can be anywhere from 970 to 1,015 crew members on board at any one time, of which approximately 20 percent are female. It is not unusual to have between 35 and 45 different nationalities represented.

The most senior person on board is the master (captain), who heads up the shipboard management team, comprised of the staff captain, chief engineer, and hotel manager. They, in turn, have the responsibility for the day-to-day administration of their respective departments. On a typical voyage the following personnel may be carried, and in most cases they will come under the jurisdiction of one of the department heads:

Able seamen 25
Accountant 1
Baggage masters 2
Bakers 5
Bank staff 3
Bartenders 17
Beauty therapist 1
Bellboys 2
Bosun 1
Butchers 3
Butlers 4
Cabin stewards 74
Cadet officers 4
Captain's secretary 1
Carpenters 5
Carpet layers 2
Cashier 1
Casino staff 16
Chefs de cuisine 5
Chefs 50
Chiropodist 1
Cinema operators 2
Classical artists 2
Cleaners 45
Clergy 2
Clerks 6
Computer systems officers 2
Cooks 44
Cruise sales manager 1
Cruise staff 16
Cruise director 1
Cunard World Club manager 1
Dancers 8
Data input clerks 2
Deck stewards 4
Dentist 1
Disc jockey 1
Dishwashers 23
Doctors 2
Dry cleaners 2

Electrical officers   6
Electrical mechanics   9
Electronic officers   2
Engine wipers   13
Engineer officers   15
Entertainers   9
Executive chef   1
Fitness instructors   6
Florists   2
Furnishing team   6
Gentlemen hosts   4
Hairdressers   12
Hotel officers   30
Interpreters   3
Joiner   1
Laundry staff   15
Lecturers   2
Librarians   2
Lift electrician   1
Linen keepers   2
Lounge stewards   24
Masseuses   4
Mechanics   42
Medical attendants   3
Motormen   15
Musicians   26
Navigating officers   9
Night stewards   4
Nursery nannies   2
Nurses   3
Painters   2
Personnel manager   1

Photographers   4
Physiotherapist   1
Pianist   1
Plumbers   4
Printers   4
Purser   1
Quartermasters   3
Radio officers   3
Receptionists   3
Refrigeration mechanics   4
Restaurant managers   21
Sanitation workers   5
Secretaries   2
Security staff   5
Security officer   1
Shop assistants   21
Social hosts   6
Spa attendants   2
Sports directors   2
Stage manager   1
Storekeepers   5
Tank cleaners   4
Technical storekeepers   2
Tours staff   3
TV station manager   1
Utility staff   25
Waiters and Waitresses   190
Wine waiters   21

The Main Control Room (MCR) was the senior watch-keeping station in the machinery spaces and was located on a deck above the main alternator room. It was air-conditioned and soundproofed. Windows looked out over the turbo alternator machinery. On the forward side were the switchboards and group starter panels for main and auxiliary machinery. The main control console housed electrical controls for the main alternator run-up schemes and various electrical circuit switching, main boiler control systems, combustion controls, main engine telegraphs, feed systems and forced draft fan controls, domestic service systems, stabilizer, and bow thruster controls. There was a comprehensive telephone and public-address system, from which, as in the Turbine Control Room, the officer had direct communications with all machinery spaces.

The Turbine Control Room, located in the engine room forward of the main turbines, had similar features to the MCR. The turbines were remotely controlled from this room, and it replaced the traditional engine maneuvering platform. All remote controls and gauges associated with the complete control of the main power plant were located in this one spot.

The original thinking that went into the machinery design dates back to 1954 when John Brown (Clydebank) was asked to prepare proposals and designs for a new ship, at that time known as the *Q3*, to replace the old *Queens*. When the order was placed for the *QE2*, the machinery was largely based on that proposed for the larger quadruple-screw ship.

Schedule requirements for a weekly transatlantic service called for an average speed of 28.5 knots, which necessitated a service shaft horsepower of between 85,000 and 95,000. In order to give a reserve of power, the main turbines were designed for a maximum output of 110,000 horsepower.

The power was shared equally between the two propellers, each driven by an independent set of turbines. The two sets of double-reduction geared turbines were supplied with steam from three high-pressure water tube boilers. Each unit was composed of a high-pressure and a double-flow low-pressure turbine which transmitted their power through dual-tandem reduction gears.

Designed by Foster Wheeler and manufactured by John Brown Engineering, the boilers were the largest ever to be fitted in a marine installation. Each boiler weighed 278 tons and was fitted with superheaters designed to operate at outlet temperatures of 1,000 degrees Fahrenheit and 850 pounds per square inch of pressure.

The propellers were attached to 250-foot-long shafts by large nuts with an internal diameter of 23 inches, which at the time were the largest ever made. The two six-bladed propellers were supplied by Stone Manganese Marine, Ltd., at a cost of over £500,000. Each weighed 31.75 tons and had a diameter of 19 feet and a pitch of 21.65 feet.

Electricity was supplied by three AEl turbine generators, each of which was capable of producing 5,500 kilowatts of power at 3,300 volts 60 hertz, and at the time they were the largest ever to be built for shipboard use.

BIBLIOGRAPHY

Albion, Robert Greenhaigh,
  Naval and Maritime History,
  Connecticut, 1963.
Anderson, Roy,
  White Star,
  Lancashire, 1964.
Angas, Commander W. Mack,
  Rivalry on the Atlantic 1833–1939,
  New York, 1939.
Appleyard, Rollo,
  Charles Parsons: His Life and Work,
  London, 1933.
Armstrong, Warren,
  Atlantic Highway,
  New York, 1962.
Arnott, Captain Robert H.,
  Captain of the Queen,
  Kent, 1982.
Aylmer, Gerald, *R.M.S. Mauretania:*
  The Ship and Her Record,
  London, 1934.
Beaudean, Baron Raoul de,
  Captain of the Ile,
  New York, 1960.
Beesley, Lawrence,
  The Loss of the S.S. Titanic,
  Boston, 1912.
Bensted, C. R.,
  Atlantic Ferry,
  London, 1936.
Bisset, Sir James,
  Ship Ahoy!
  London, 1932.
  Sail Ho,
  London, 1958.
  Tramps and Ladies,
  London, 1959.
  Commodore,
  New York, 1961.

Bonsor, N.R.P.,
  North Atlantic Seaway,
  Channel Islands, 1980.
  South Atlantic Seaway,
  Channel Islands, 1983.
Bowen, Frank C., *A Century of*
  Atlantic Travel 1830–1930,
  Boston, 1930.
Brady, Edward Michael,
  Marine Salvage Operations,
  New York, 1960.
Braynard, Frank O.,
  By Their Work Ye Shall Know Them,
  New York, 1968.
Brinnin, John Malcolm,
  The Sway of the Grand Saloon,
  New York, 1971.
Broakes, Nigel,
  A Growing Concern,
  London, 1979.
Buchanan, Gary,
  Dream Voyages,
  Jersey, 1989.
Corson, F. Reid, *The Atlantic Ferry*
  in the Twentieth Century,
  London, 1930.
Cunard Line,
  The Cunarders 1840–1969: A Transatlantic
  Story Spanning 129 Years,
  London, 1969.
Dunn, Laurence,
  North Atlantic Liners: 1899–1913,
  London, 1961.
Dunnett, Alastair M.,
  The Donaldson Line: 1854–1954,
  Glasgow, 1960.
Fry, Henry, *The History of*
  North Atlantic Steam Navigation,
  London, 1896.

Gibbs, C.R. Vernon,
  Passenger Liners of the Western Ocean,
  London, 1957.
  *British Passenger Liners of
  the Five Oceans*,
  London, 1963.
Grattidge, Harvey,
  Captain of the Queens,
  New York, 1956.
Hoehling, Adolph, and Mary Hoehling,
  The Last Voyage of the Lusitania,
  New York, 1956.
Hutchings, David F.,
  QE2 — A Ship for all Seasons,
  Southampton, 1987.
Hyde, Francis E.,
  Cunard and the North Atlantic: 1840–1972,
  London, 1975
Isherwood, J.H.,
  Steamers of the Past,
  Liverpool, 1966.
Johnson, Howard,
  The Cunard Story,
  London, 1987.
Kludas, Arnold, *Great Passenger
  Ships of the World*,
  Cambridge, 1975.
Lauriat, Charles E.,
  The Lusitania's Last Voyage,
  New York, 1915.
Lee, Charles E.,
  The Blue Riband,
  London, 1930.
Lindsay, W.S.,
  History of Merchant Shipping,
  London, 1876.
Lloyd, Wertf, *Queen Elizabeth 2 —
  The Story of a Conversion*
  Bremerhaven, 1976.
Lord, Walter,
  A Night to Remember,
  New York, 1955.
Lowdnes, Russ, *Samuel Cunard
  Bicentennial: 1787–1987*
  Halifax, Canada, 1987.
Maber, John,
  North Star to Southern Cross,
  Lancashire, 1967.
McCart, Neil,
  Atlantic Liners of the Cunard Line,
  London, 1990.
McLennan, R.S.,
  Anchor Line: 1856–1956,
  Glasgow, 1956.
Maginnis, A.J.,
  The Atlantic Ferry,
  London, 1900.

Maxtone-Graham, John,
  The Only Way to Cross,
  New York, 1972.
  Cunard — 150 Glorious Years,
  Devon, 1989.
Moody, Bert,
  Ocean Ships,
  London, 1971.
Moxom, Peter M. Fimister, and A.
Burney,
  QE2 — Cunard's Flagship,
  Surrey, 1990.
Oldham, Wilton J.,
  The Ismay Line,
  Liverpool, 1961.
Potter, Neil, and Jack Frost,
  The Mary,
  London, 1961.
  The Elizabeth,
  London, 1965.
  The Queen Elizabeth 2,
  London, 1969.
Preble, Rear-Admiral G.H.,
  History of Steam Navigation,
  Philadelphia, 1883.
Shaum, John H. Jr., and William
H. Flayhart III,
  *Majesty at Sea: The Four
  Funnel Liners*,
  New York, 1981.
Smallpeice, Sir Basil,
  Of Comets and Queens,
  Shrewsbury, 1980.
Smith, Eugene W.,
  *Passenger Ships of the World — Past
  and Present*,
  Boston, 1963.
Spedding, Charles T.,
  *Reminiscenses of TransAtlantic Trav-
  elers*
  Philadelphia, 1926.
Staff, Frank,
  The Trans-Atlantic Mail,
  London, 1956.
Stevens, Leonard A.,
  The El;izabeth: Passage of a Queen,
  New York, 1968.
Thomas, David St. John,
  The Cunard Book of Cruising,
  Devon, 1990.
Winberg, William M.,
  QE2 — The Official Pictorial History,
  California, 1988.

INDEX

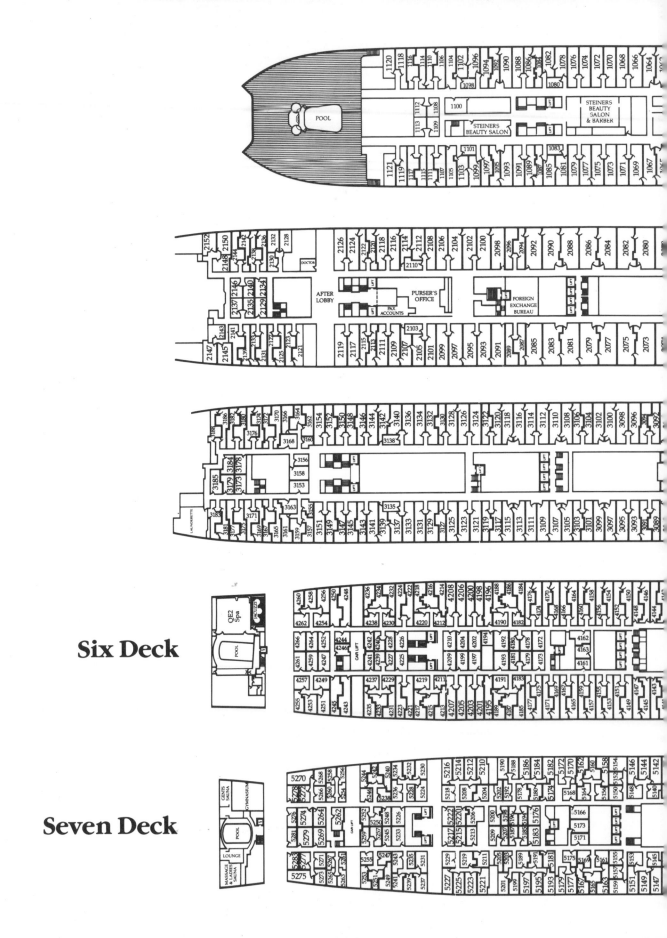

Six Deck

Seven Deck